Following a BA Hons degree in English Literature, Alasdair Moore became a gardener at Queen's Park in London. In 1992 he was awarded the annual studentship at the renowned Tresco Abbey Gardens, Isles of Scilly, before training at the Royal Horticultural Society, Wisley. He worked with the National Trust and Marilyn Abbot at West Green House in Hampshire until 1995, when he returned to Tresco Abbey Gardens as Assistant-Head Gardener until 2003. In 1997 Moore was the recipient of a Winston Churchill Fellowship to study the Protea family in South Africa, the flora of which is his particular passion. He has led a series of garden tours to the Riviera, Madeira and South Africa as well as lecturing at The Royal Botanic Gardens, Kew, where he also achieved a diploma in Botanic Garden Management. Moore is a regular contributor to *Gardens Illustrated* and has written about gardening for the *Independent on Saturday* and the *Daily Telegraph*.

# La Mortola

*For my parents,*
*Richard and Sheila*

# La Mortola

in the footsteps of
Thomas Hanbury

*Alasdair Moore*

To Alex on
the Riviera

Alasdair
Moore

**CADOGAN**

Cadogan Guides
Highlands House, 165 The Broadway, Wimbledon, London SW19 1NE
info@cadoganguides.co.uk
www.cadoganguides.com

The Globe Pequot Press
246 Goose Lane, PO Box 480, Guilford,
Connecticut 06437–0480

Printed in Italy by Legoprint
A catalogue record for this book is available
from the British Library
ISBN: 1-8601-11408

# Contents

# Introduction

In the early spring of 1907 a funeral took place in the Italian town of San Remo. The funeral cortège brought the body from the small village of La Mortola, some 15 miles away along the Ligurian coast. As the carriages made their way to San Remo through the towns and villages, shops closed and people stood in silence. Many of these respectful bystanders then fell in behind the procession and accompanied the cortège to the church. It was estimated that some 7,000 people were following on foot by the time that the coffin reached San Remo. The subject of this reverence was not an Italian dignitary or saintly padre, but an Englishman, a native not of Imperia but of Clapham and a Quaker by faith. His name was Sir Thomas Hanbury.

Sir Thomas had lived in Italy for the last 40 years of his life, and the affection felt for him by the people of his adopted home was the result of his great charity, providing schools, fountains, jobs, medical assistance for the poor, and even a botanical institute. As a young man he had lived in Shanghai and there he had made an immense fortune, amid the great anarchy of mid-19th century China, before returning to Europe. At La Mortola Thomas (as we shall call him from now on) created one of the finest gardens and plant collections ever assembled, of which Sir Joseph Hooker, Director of Kew, wrote in 1893: 'in point of richness and interest, [it] has no rival amongst the private collections of living plants in the world'. Thomas Hanbury was knighted by King Edward VII and decorated by the Italian state. Thomas's life was one that spanned continents and revolutions, but his achievements are not widely known today. Indeed few people even recognize this great Victorian's name. Those that do tend to be gardeners and it was only as a gardener myself, or rather as a student gardener that I was first to become aware of Thomas Hanbury.

There are several fine horticultural colleges in Britain but if you were to ask a lay person to name any of them the chances are that two, above all others, would be mentioned: Kew and Wisley. If the horticultural institutions of Britain can be likened to the hierarchy of the Christian faith, then the Royal Botanic Garden at Kew is the Pope, while the garden of the Royal Horticultural Society (RHS) at Wisley makes for an excellent Archbishop of Canterbury. Rightly or wrongly, these pillars of the horticultural establishment are perceived by many to be the most prestigious in the country. Horticultural snobs would argue that a gardener's CV lacking the presence of either Kew or Wisley, while not naked, could be described as somewhat underdressed. In 1993, in an attempt to lower the odds, I applied to both. Kew, sadly, decided that I was not to be part of its flock but, much to my relief, Wisley was not going to turn me away from its door.

I have many reasons to thank Wisley. Wisley and its staff taught me a great deal about gardening and about plants. Even on the odd occasion when I brought a little too much of the previous evening's conviviality to work the next morning, patience and good humour seemed abundant. I am grateful for my time at Wisley as I write these words, for it was at Wisley that I first heard the name of Thomas

Hanbury. The inevitable student induction day was a typical and relentless procession of people, aims, rules, expectations and tradition. A brief lecture on the history of the RHS was delivered, during which it was explained that the reason why this noble society was educating us novices in a mock-Jacobean mansion in the depths of Surrey was down to the generosity of Thomas Hanbury. Six hundred and fifty thousand people a year pass through the gates of Wisley, the splendid flagship garden of the RHS. Since the beginning of the 20th century Wisley has represented the best of British horticulture, and the gardens have been a source of pleasure and knowledge for millions of visitors. During that time only a few of that vast host of garden enthusiasts would have recognized the name of Thomas Hanbury, yet without him their enjoyment of Wisley would have been impossible. Thomas Hanbury bought Wisley in 1903 and donated it to the RHS. This generous act came at a crucial time for the RHS and it was one that helped to ensure the future prosperity of the society. The importance of Thomas to the history of the RHS is plain, but the gift of Wisley is far from being the sum of his life

As a consequence of my disregard for even the most basic principles of accounting, my education with the RHS was cut short and I left before completing the course. I had been offered a position as an assistant gardener at West Green House in Hampshire and the lure of regular income above my student rate proved too much to resist. A compact 18th-century country house owned by the National Trust but available on lease, West Green House had a fascinating garden to work in. The previous incumbent of the house had been Lord McAlpine of West Green. McAlpine had enjoyed part of his education at Stowe in Buckingham and it was from the school's historic estate that he had formed an appreciation of the late 17th- and

18th-century styles of garden and landscape design. The grounds of West Green House, therefore, were liberally sprinkled with various follies, monuments and architectural conceits. McAlpine liked his garden to have the same air of genteel decay that Stowe had in its pre-National Trust days, a landscape marooned in a picturesque no man's land that lay indistinctly between the wild and the kempt.

At the end of the 1980s McAlpine moved on. This artful garden that had teetered theatrically on the brink of disrepair deteriorated rapidly once it was left untended. The natural vegetation, after years of being held straining at the leash, launched itself on the garden in an exuberant riot. Trees vanished from sight under thick and sinuous briar and brambles, ash saplings sprang up on paths, ditches choked, and the lake was transformed into a marshy lawn. Once during my time there McAlpine came to see what had become of his garden. He was returning from a Tory party conference and in passing he had been unable to resist instructing his chauffeur to drop by West Green House. His dismay at the garden's restoration programme was not concealed. I remember that the word 'ruined' was particularly favoured and his distaste seemed suffused with melancholy.

Lord McAlpine arrived at the bleakest point in the garden's regeneration and I could well understand his sadness. None of his structures had been removed and the bones of the garden that he had so carefully laid out were still evident, but the vital spirit of his garden had gone. The new leaseholder was Marilyn Abbott, whose resplendent designs and vision for the garden at West Green House were incompatible with McAlpine's preference for crumbling elegance. The regimen of the potager was to spill out of the confines of the walled garden, and into the little orchards, meadows and alleys that surrounded it. The clearance work, after five years of neglect, was very great indeed. There was no possibility of cosmetic surgery. With our saws and secateurs, the gardeners cut out the heart of McAlpine's garden.

No one ever truly owns a garden, it is said, but gardens are certainly all about the people who make them. A lot of gardens are exercises in approved aesthetics and social preening. This is not a dismissal of gardens, nor is it merely cynicism. The garden demonstrates wealth and taste in one of the most public of displays. What really makes a garden distinguished is the manner in which an individual expresses these elements; in a way, how people imprint themselves and their personalities upon a garden. McAlpine's garden was one made in his own image; it was particular to him. That garden had huge personality and, as such, once McAlpine left it was condemned to become a memory. The garden had been given a most specific agenda, one that was unlikely to be sustained by the next resident at West Green. West Green now has another beautiful garden, courtesy of Marilyn Abbott. The more personal one makes a garden, the more tenuous one's hold is on its future. Adjustment and rearrangement can change a garden's nature and its meaning.

The garden at West Green and its weight of personal expression formed a stark contrast to the committee-laden and public nature of Wisley. The garden that Thomas gave to the RHS is impersonal, it is not the product of a single vision; and its owners, the members of the RHS, number around 300,000. The purpose of McAlpine's West Green was personal pleasure, while the fundamental aim of Wisley is to inform the multitude. The harmonious balance of private and public within a garden is a rare accomplishment, one admirably achieved by Thomas at his own garden at La Mortola.

Gardens have always depended on the actions and vision of powerful and imaginative personalities. The Abbey Gardens on Tresco, one of the Isles of Scilly, is just such a garden. The year prior to my time at Wisley I was awarded the annual studentship to Tresco. The 12 months that I spent in its handsome exotic garden were a profoundly formative period in my education as a gardener. When I left West Green House, it was to Tresco that I returned. The Isles of Scilly lie off the furthermost tip of Southwest England, some 24 miles from the jagged rocks of Land's End. The islands are a low-lying cluster of granite rocks, too numerous to name, of which five are inhabited. Set in clear waters and edged by beaches of clean white sand, the Isles of Scilly remain for me the most beautiful place that I have ever seen. Their geographical location provides the islands with the most temperate climate in the British Isles. Frosts are few and far between, the average winter temperature seldom dropping below 3°C. This does not prevent the islands from regularly being battered by howling Atlantic gales during the winter months, but for the gardener these winds are the only real enemy.

When Augustus Smith established himself on the islands in 1834, he soon realized the horticultural potential of the islands. He had come to the Isles of Scilly as a wealthy and principled young man, determined to put his fortune to good use. Smith took on the lease of the islands from the Duchy of Cornwall, becoming Lord Proprietor of the Isles of Scilly. For nearly forty years he spent his energies and his money on the improvement of the islands. He chose the island of Tresco on which to build his house. Tresco is the most sheltered of all the islands, protected on three sides by the islands of St Martin's, St Mary's and Bryher. It was on Tresco that the Benedictine monks sited their priory in the early 12th century, a sure sign of the superior nature of the location. Smith placed his own home, christened the Abbey, adjacent to the ruins of this priory.

Augustus Smith, though striving for the betterment of the islands and their inhabitants, was a figure of considerable authority, an authority not always welcomed and frequently resented. He was known as 'the Emperor' or 'the Governor' by friends and enemies alike; nicknames that may help to shed some light on his management style. On the Isles of Scilly his power was unchallenged and his philanthropy was aggressive. Typical of his Benthamite attitude to improving the lot of his employees and their families was his introduction of compulsory schooling. Parents were charged a penny a week for the attendance of each of their children and twopence for truancy. It was not unknown for the Emperor to engender some enthusiasm for education in absentees with the help of a stick.

In 1866 Augustus Smith became embroiled in a dispute that further illustrates the nature of the man. Smith, previously to his role as Lord Proprietor, had maintained an interest in the welfare of the poor who lived in the area surrounding his family's estate of Ashlyns, near Berkhamsted. A confrontation arose between Smith and Lord Brownlow concerning Berkhamsted Common. In February 1866 Brownlow forced the issue further by summarily enclosing 600 acres of common land behind a fence of stout iron railings. Smith was incensed by this deliberate infringement of the rights of the local poor. He chartered a train to leave Euston Station filled with workmen. It left on the night of 5 March and arrived at Tring, from where the workmen walked the three miles to Berkhamsted Common. By seven o' clock the next morning the workmen had gone and the iron railings were lying in tidy piles around the boundary of those disputed 600 acres. A painstaking legal battle then began. It lasted four expensive and infuriating years, at the end of which the rights of the poor were upheld.

In taking on responsibility for a rural area such as the Isles of Scilly, Smith was aware of current agricultural practices. One of his earliest and least popular edicts was the introduction of a system of primogeniture, to put an end to the progressive division of available farm land into smaller and smaller parcels. The prevalence of these fields, too small to yield a viable crop and unsuitable grazing, had led to a crisis in farming on the islands. The agricultural difficulties on the islands were not limited to questions of inheritance. Despite the absence of frost, the exposure to the strong, salt-laden gales proved extremely troublesome. Hundreds of years previously the islands had been wooded, but since the arrival of human beings all these trees had been cleared for land use or for firewood. At the time of Augustus Smith's arrival there was not a single tree anywhere on the islands. The establishment of an effective natural shelterbelt remained a priority for Smith and his descendants.

Early on in this process of planting Smith came to understand that the benign temperatures afforded by the islands would allow for the cultivation of exotic plants that would be unable to survive on cooler, mainland Britain. By the early 1840s he had begun to plant up the ruins of the old priory in the grounds of his house. The crumbling stone walls that had stood for centuries offered vital shelter for young plants in the treeless environment. The soil was thin, dark and acidic. This poor, free-draining medium, in tandem with the sloping and rocky topography of the land around the priory, made for a perfect setting for an experimental garden.

Succulent plants, in particular, caught Smith's imagination. Mesembryanthemum, or 'Mesmerisms' as Smith referred to them, were particular favourites. These low-growing natives of South Africa, now divided into many separate genera, have small, fleshy leaves, like swollen grains of rice, on thin woody stems. Their robust root systems, used to the hardships of arid South African summers, mean that they grow well in the cracks in walls or in shallow pockets of soil on a cliff face. A mature plant can cover a square metre, and in late spring and summer the plant disappears under a thick mass of iridescent flowers. Each bloom is a multitude of soft, thin petals, ranging in colour from soft lilacs to eye-watering reds and yellows. Through the unusual beauty of his 'Mesmerisms' and other plants, Augustus Smith became increasingly devoted to, and proud of, his garden.

Augustus Smith died in 1872, but successive generations of his family, later known as the Dorrien-Smiths, have continued to develop Tresco socially and economically, having returned the lease for all the other inhabited islands in the group to the Duchy of Cornwall in 1922. The benevolence and forward thinking that characterized Augustus Smith was carried on by his descendants. The garden too continued to expand and today it is not only one of the most important draws for visitors to the islands, but is one of Britain's foremost gardens.

My return to Tresco and its garden coincided with the development of links between the Abbey Gardens and an Italian garden by the name of La Mortola. La Mortola, as I was soon to discover, was the garden that Thomas had spent more than half his life building, planting and developing. By the time of his death, in 1907, La Mortola was renowned as one of the finest plant collections in Europe, set in one of Europe's most beautiful gardens. The gift of Wisley to the RHS was a transfer of real estate, a matter of the purse. La Mortola was a matter of the heart.

Tresco's curator, Mike Nelhams, had nurtured the idea of a link between the two gardens for some time. As he spoke of the garden and the Hanbury family, a picture of Thomas began to form in my mind. Thomas, it appeared to me, had spent his days in the idyllic endeavour of making a garden on the Riviera. He had endless amounts of the two most important ingredients for the great garden recipe: money and time. I saw him wafting through his garden (straw boater, walking stick, linen suit, mutton-chop whiskers) offering encouragement to his cheery local gardeners, before drifting back to the palazzo for a pink gin and a spot of lunch, and spending a life in retirement, free from worry and set apart from the seamier aspects of the world, such as real work and hardship. This childish caricature had no past and in my mind existed, not in the second half of the 19th century, but in some timeless Riviera netherworld of Scott Fitzgerald, Cary Grant and Grace Kelly.

Thomas himself made the initial link between Tresco and La Mortola. Having entertained a member of the Dorrien-Smith family to lunch at La Mortola in 1901, Thomas spent a weekend on Tresco in July 1902. Thomas, it seems, had rather underestimated the horticultural achievements of the Dorrien-Smiths. His diary entry for 12 July reads: 'Very delighted with the vegetation in garden of Tresco Abbey. Much exceeds my expectation.' The hospitality of the Dorrien-Smiths may have proved too much for Thomas, as he notes on the final day of his visit that one of the smaller islands was '…swarming with penguins and gulls'. (It is safe to surmise that Thomas meant to write 'puffins' rather than 'penguins'.) I saw in a luscious coffee-table book about gardens by the sea that a similar confusion had occurred between Tresco and La Mortola. The author asserted that the gardens at Tresco had been begun by a fictitious hybrid called August Hambury. Augustus and Thomas shared more than just an interest in exotic flora. They were both determined, successful men with a strong sense of social responsibility, whose gardens existed as parts of communities larger than simply their households. The gardens have a commonality both real and imagined.

My first visit to the Hanbury Gardens at La Mortola was as a tour guide for a group of very forgiving garden enthusiasts. The tour was based in Nice, from where we made daily forays into the surrounding area. My expert knowledge of the Riviera and its gardens depended on a week's holiday that I had enjoyed there as a 13-year-old boy, at a time in my life when plants and gardens offered only a possible source of concealment from parents. Even if I had been one of those faintly worrying horticultural prodigies, that holiday, with the exception of the drive to and from the airport, had been spent entirely on a boat. I am glad to say that my plant knowledge, at least, had improved since those childhood days, a result, perhaps, of hiding in all those bushes. In any case, La Mortola, the grand finale of the four-day tour, rather spoke for itself. I found myself entranced. It is not a pristine, manicured garden: it is a garden still surviving on the fat laid down from years before. La Mortola is a feast, however, for those who love plants, for those who love both scale and detail, for those who feel nobility in a garden, for those to whom a garden is more than just a room to be decorated, and for those whose response to a garden is not based on good housekeeping. La Mortola is a garden of greatness. My interest in Thomas Hanbury began to develop. As a tour leader I returned several more times: each time the stature of La Mortola grew, as did my fascination with it.

In 1999 Mike Nelhams informed the gardeners at the Abbey Gardens that we were all to go to Italy for one week in February. We would stay in the villa owned by Carolyn Hanbury, situated in the gardens at La Mortola. We would spend the mornings working in her garden, and the afternoons visiting the numerous gardens and plant collections in the area. This was an arrangement that recurred for the next three years. It is from these visits that this book really stems. Carolyn had first come to live at La Mortola in 1995 with her husband, Simon Hanbury. Simon, a great-grandson of Thomas, had inherited Casa Nirvana in 1993. Simon was passionately fond of La Mortola, where he had spent every summer holiday of his youth. Tragically, Simon died of cancer in 1997. Carolyn continues to work tirelessly on behalf of the garden and maintains the Hanbury presence at La Mortola. It was from listening to Carolyn talk about Thomas that I began to understand what an extraordinary man he was.

This is not simply a tale of a gentleman gardener whiling away his days on the shores of the Mediterranean. Here is a narrative grand in scale: how he acquired an enormous fortune in China as 2,000 years of civilization fell apart around him; how he came to Italy just as that nation was being born; how it is that streets are named after him in Italian towns; and how he came to found the first and foremost great garden of the Riviera. Thomas Hanbury spent his adult life, not in the relative security and stability of Victorian Britain, but in the raw atmosphere of change and revolution that characterizes the 19th century. The genial old buffer whom I had first imagined was on hand at the rise and fall of nations. At a point of history when principles and charity seemed to be threatened with extinction, Thomas Hanbury proved himself more than equal to the great traditions of his faith. He was not, however, a cold embodiment of saintliness, but a man attempting to live up to the high moral standards that he set himself. His life was not without moral dilemmas and choices that he may have regretted making. He remains an outstanding human being.

This book does not claim to be a definitive work, nor does it adhere to a strict chronology. Rather, it is an attempt to win greater recognition for Sir Thomas Hanbury and his achievements, by offering a sense of the man and his time. The garden is central to this book, but I hope to take Thomas out of the garden and to place him in a broader historical context. I want to investigate how Thomas came to make such an important garden at La Mortola, and the impression he made upon this unequalled coast.

# Chapter One
# La Mortola: Giardini Hanbury

A casual tourist could be forgiven for missing the entrance to the Hanbury Gardens at La Mortola. Entering Italy from Menton, following the lower corniche, the tourist is almost immediately plunged into the La Mortola tunnel, which runs underneath the garden itself. The driver has passed the garden already. The large sign, however, that steers the inquisitive off the busy coastal road and up the snaking Corso Monte Carlo to the '*Giardini Botanici Hanbury*' is certainly hard to ignore. There begins the climb up the meandering road to the southern edge of the village of La Mortola Inferiore. The hillside that rises up out of the Mediterranean is typical of the area. Its most precipitous slopes are clear of buildings, but from the corniche upwards the face of the hill is dotted irregularly with houses and villas seemingly pinned to the rock. The shuttered houses, brightly coloured in earthy pinks and oranges, are scattered on terraces crowded with vegetation, some producing fruit and some purely ornamental. The road is steeply embanked with pale limestone walls, whose pointing is regularly augmented by the roots and stems of opportunistic plants. Prickly pears, wigandias and great bursts of pink bougainvillea spring forth from these roadside walls. The greys of olive, eucalyptus and evergreen oak are matched by the greens of slender cypresses and pines. Below, the great bay that curves round from Cap Saint Martin in France to Bordighera in Italy falls further away.

As the road rounds yet another corner, the pastel clock tower of San Mauro Church appears, standing clear of the terracotta roofs and the crowns of the trees. Just below the tower, right on the side of the road is a small pink house with green shutters. On its upper storey is mounted a large wooden sign, its faded green paint revealing the legend:

*Riviera Dei Fiori*
*La Mortola*
*Giardini Hanbury.*

The road bends sharply to the right. As a result there is little chance of seeing the thin, graffitied sign among the olive branches that once read '*Giardini Hanbury Ingresso*', but behind the grey iron railing fence flickers the green promise of a garden. A handsome and sturdy stone archway provides the garden entrance. There is no car park, only a handful of berths for residents and visitors alike at the side of the road. To the left, through the railings, the ground drops away, revealing a canopy of palm trees and eucalypts.

The entrance to the Hanbury Gardens is the most dramatic and effective entrance to any garden that I have ever visited. The gateway is a fine and substantial archway, with two small ante-rooms to each side. The style speaks of stolid grandeur. As you approach the entrance, it is possible to see through the railings, down onto the tree canopy within and across the narrow valley that cradles the garden to the barren ridge that marks its western boundary. To the left as one passes through the arch is the ticket booth. Buy your ticket and then return back out through the arch, to the edge of the road. If you have the inclination and the patience, wait for any other visitors to go on their way. What greets you through the entrance is a parcel of blue, framed by the dark verticals of a narrow corridor of cypress and the gentle curve of the arch itself. The best position to appreciate this is standing opposite the portal on the far side of the road – but beware of the traffic, which hurls itself lethally around the corner.

The sea and the sky are the greatest backdrop for any garden and for any plant. The sea and the sky bring a sense of indefinite space to a garden, however small its actual dimensions: they seem to me to set plants free. Their blues serve as a natural ha-ha, making the garden wall redundant. That moment of pure blue, the blue of the sea as you enter the garden, does not last long, but it leads you into the green and beyond, for the sea is where the garden ends.

Steep steps bordered by the cypress trees take you down to the garden path. Immediately one is aware of the gradient on which the garden is constructed, descending sharply to the rocky promontory and shore far below. The flight of stairs is broken into three smaller stages, each punctuated by pelargoniums in pots, and, with each downward step, the canvas of sea, sky and garden deepens. At the top of the final set of steps the Palazzo Orengo emerges, its single tower poking through the cypress, pines and palms. The palazzo stands on a site inhabited by man for hundreds of years and the building itself dates back to the 17th century. Its current form of restrained elegance is the result of renovations and additions made by Thomas Hanbury. The Palazzo Orengo was the home of Thomas and his family. Its beautiful ochre-washed walls are partly obscured by the layered branches of an araucaria, a relative of the monkey-puzzle tree, whose dark evergreen leaves highlight the tones of the building. At the foot of the stairway two elderly olive trees mark the end of the avenue of cypress. The pale grey underside of the olives' small, muted green leaves, set in pairs along whitish stems, put silver into the shade of the cypress.

The profound resonance that this garden emanates is dependent upon the cypress and the olive. These emblems of the Mediterranean form a vital thematic element to La Mortola, providing vegetative, cultural and historical continuity with the greater landscape. Both trees have been growing on this site for hundreds, perhaps thousands, of years.

The olive, *Olea europaea*, is possibly the commonest cultivated tree along the Riviera. Despite many of the ancient groves being lost to developments of housing and other forms of cultivation, the rounded grey crowns of olive trees still give many of the local hillsides their characteristic sheen. The olive has been the Mediterranean's tree of life for as long as human beings have had the intellectual capacity to eat its fruit and use its wood. The natural resilience of the olive tree is legendary: hacked to the most rudimentary framework for its fruit each year, the olive brings forth a mass of new branches. It was said that an area that could normally provide subsistence for one family could sustain 20 families if it was planted with olive groves. There is no doubt of the economic importance of the olive, particularly for the villages away from the coast, and it was a trade that saw a huge expansion in Liguria during the Napoleonic period.

Thomas Hanbury built a guest house at the edge of his property called Casa Nirvana. It was here that I was fortunate enough to stay while writing much of this book and where I enjoyed the considerable hospitality of Carolyn Hanbury. The olive trees in the private garden of Casa Nirvana once formed part of the grove that runs through the Hanbury Garden. Some of these olives are of an incalculable antiquity: specimens whose heartwood has rotted out to leave a shell of sinuous wood and bark twisting around the hollow that remains. There are other ancient trees whose new trunks emerge, not from the soil, but from swollen rootstocks spread across the ground. These can be metres in circumference, forming grey mounds like the cooled deposits of lignified lava. From the story of Noah to the stumbling peace process between Israel and Palestine the olive branch has permeated the culture of Europe and the Mediterranean as a symbol of peace, of new beginnings. The potential for new beginnings is endless for the olive. Its lust for life is irrepressible and of deep significance to man.

If the olive tree represents life, then the tall and slim elegance of the cypress, *Cupressus sempervirens*, has attained a symbolic stature of a darker hue. The association between death and the cypress is an ancient one. An unmistakable element of the Italian landscape, the cypress was the tree of Pluto, god of the Underworld. The tree was often planted in cemeteries. In Greece and Egypt the cypress's tough wood, resistant to decay and insects, was used for coffins, while it may also have been the source for the 'gopher wood' of Noah's Ark.

Thomas's appreciation of the natural world of the Riviera and its relationship with man was extensive. In an act typical of his enthusiasm and generosity he paid for the publication in 1903 of a book on that very subject. Its title was *Riviera Nature Notes*. Its author, the Reverend C. Casey, relates:

The cypress is one of those plants termed 'cosmogonic': it is a Tree of Life, and at the same time a Tree of Death. This is why the drowning world was saved in a coffer made of imperishable Gopher wood. I believe the Ark or chest that bore Danaë and her babe across the sea from Argos to the Cyclades was of this same sacred wood. But, on the other hand, the 'funereal Cypress' is dedicated to Pluto, and planted by the tombs of the departed. The discovery was made in very early times that life and death are complementary, that the greatest blessing may be the greatest bane, and vice versa.

The superstitious dread of the Cypress still lingers among the peasantry near Nice. I wished to plant a few of these trees at one end of my garden to give shade; but the gardener, an honest and good-hearted old man, begged me not to meddle with them.

'You will suffer,' he said, 'if you plant a Cypress.' Thinking that he was afraid on his own account, I asked him to dig them up and bring them: I would plant them myself. I might as well have asked him to bring a tiger and let it loose in the garden![1]

The olive and the cypress share a rich heritage, not least their links to the story of Noah. They are both used extensively in gardens on the Riviera. Many properties have been built on the sites of old olive groves, and the beautiful and eccentric forms of the olives have been incorporated into the gardens. A most memorable example of this is at Les Colombiers, which is to be found in Garavan, behind Menton. This recently restored private garden is both fascinating and charming. At one point, near to the house, a flight of stone steps leads one down into an olive grove. Towards the end of this run of steps there stands an olive tree. The stonework has been constructed around the base of this venerable tree and the stairway continues on without a break. The effect is not only visually arresting but also poetic: a garden haiku. Together the olive and the cypress are a familiar and attractive planting combination, with their rounded greys and vertical greens complementing each other splendidly.

At La Mortola, I believe, their double act preserves the unity of a garden that is characterized by diversity and innovation. The Hanbury Gardens are a botanic cocktail, packed with plants from as far a field as China, Mexico, Madagascar and Australia. The cypress and the olive supply a controlling influence on what might otherwise be too heady a brew. They are not alone in doing this job of tempering the exotic with the Mediterranean, for the pines, evergreen oaks and carobs work to this end as well. From the entrance, however, the cypress and the olive set the pace. They were vital from the beginning in structuring the garden physically, protecting plants and soil. Some of these trees were subject to judicious thinning in order to make way for the garden, but the continued presence of the cypress and the olive was unquestioned. Aesthetically, they act as a filter for the eye, helping the exotic plants to sit comfortably within the Mediterranean landscape. Spiritually, they confer on the garden the calmness of longevity and the continuity of human experience.

At the bottom of the entrance steps the short avenue of cypress ends with a flourish of olive. They mark the end of the traditional, of the familiar. In the foreground now is foliage from distant lands: large, banana-like leaves of *Strelitzia nicholii*, a huge bird of paradise plant from South Africa, that can grow more than 15 metres high, with white flowers 50 centimetres long, and the fine foliage of the jacaranda tree, whose gorgeous lilac blue flowers melt into the sky line in June. The botanic garden has begun. The path then curves down to the left within a few metres of the last step. On one side the angular, spiked heads of the tree-like *Yucca elephantipes* edge the path and bring it round past the strelitzias. The opposite bank that rises above the path is secured firmly by the roots of olive trees, below which sits a drift of *Aloe x principis*. Aloes have whorls of pointed succulent leaves held in rosettes and this specimen is like a shrub of starfish. In the spring these rosettes send up erect stems topped with flower heads of deep reds and orange. The rearmost members of this group of aloes intermingle with the roots of the olives. They are not native to this coast of the Mediterranean; the lineage of *Aloe x principis* is South African. In the clefts of the rootstock of this olive tree there are aloes growing. So embedded are these aloes that they appear to be sprouting from the stock of the olive. This to me is one of the defining images of La Mortola: a précis of the garden's style, written in plants.

The path turns again and leads on to a junction, where it divides in two. The vista now unfolds as the wide horizon of the Mediterranean stretches out, broken only by the elegant spires of cypress. The bowed vantage point provided here gives the first and best opportunity to survey the layout and topography of the garden. The cape of La Mortola is a strip of land that runs down to the sea roughly in a north–south orientation and the terraced garden fills this cape. The verdant hillside draws the eye south, down through the olives, palms and cypress to the sea. Right at the bottom it is possible to make out the clutch of *Pinus pinaster* that marks the garden's frontier with the sea. A thick musk of pine hangs heavily about these resinous trees and it is the distinctive incense of the landscape. Looking immediately down, the ground plunges away into the shallow valley, but also to the shore. Beneath the canopy of palms the under-planting has become visible, most notably the agaves, aloes and dasylirions on the slopes and further down the Vialle di Cycas, the Cycad Walk. Also apparent are the number of meandering paths and the choices they create.

To gain entrance to the Hanbury Gardens the visitor has to come in at the northeastern tip of the garden. The eastern boundary of the garden follows the Discesa del Marinaio, an old fisherman's path, down to the sea and its grey pebble beaches. The viewing terrace is only a few metres from this ancient right of way, which passes under some houses on the perimeter. This vantage point, therefore, looks directly west, across a canopy of palms and the narrowest part of the garden to its opposite boundary. This western boundary is the ridge of the Valle Sorbo. The Sorbo is a seasonal stream whose valley holds the western half of the garden. The valley and lower portions of the ridge have a wild air about them, and are thick with pines and eucalyptus. The more precipitous parts of the ridge are without vegetation, exposing a creamy limestone. Silhouetted on its crest runs the perimeter fence. The upper parts are clothed in shrubby garrigue, rosemary, spurge and cistus. This tough scrub represents the native flora of the region, but its presence on these outer reaches of the Hanbury property today is far from being a natural inevitability.

Thomas Hanbury's interest in plants was not confined to the exotic. In 1867, when he arrived at La Mortola, these rocky slopes had been stripped bare by the depredations of man and beast. The demands for firewood and fodder had made the ridge quite clean of vegetation. It was Thomas and his eldest brother, Daniel, who reintroduced native species of tree and shrub to the western border of the garden. Their actions seem prescient of today's increased appreciation of the natural environment. Thomas Hanbury, botanist and gardener, saw worth and beauty in a breadth of plants that reflects that his interests were not shackled to traditional aesthetics. He looked to preserve a flora that was diminishing around the populated coast, and he was pragmatic enough to know what would grow on these harsh and exposed extremities. The exuberance of this great collection of plants from around the world was calmed by the restraint imposed by the plants native to the Riviera.

Between these eastern and the western points is, therefore, the core of the garden's upper portion. Immediately below the terrace the land drops away into the valley but also plunges south, down towards the sea. This eastern slope is littered with a superb collection of succulent plants from Africa and the Americas, capable of withstanding the intense dryness and solar radiation of the summer months. Up the valley lie the gardeners' potting sheds and the northern boundary, which is the continuation of the road winding up from the hill from the coast. To the eye, however, there are only endless shades of green.

There are two paths leading from this vantage point. To the left lies the eastern edge of the garden, with banks and terraces thick with aloes, agaves, yuccas and cacti. This style of planting is most popular for the display of succulent plants in gardens around the world and it is one that almost certainly found its first expression in the gardens of La Mortola. This route branches and divides but, inevitably, its final destination is the sea.

The path leading to the right gently drops down to the palazzo. It is fringed with palm trees, planted by Thomas and his palm-besotted head-gardener, Ludwig Winter. Phoenix, brahea, trachycarpus, livistonia, washingtonia, jubaea and chamaerops species were used abundantly in the garden's structure. The palms are old and bear the scars of Europe's fraught past. Shrapnel from shells fired in the Second World War has gouged and torn holes into their trunks. Their survival is a testament to the equanimity of nature: there is even a shell-hole in one palm that has become the roost of owls.

The edge of this avenue down to the palazzo is planted with the purple-flowered *Salvia leucantha*. Beyond this border, beneath the palms, grow a variety of small trees and shrubs, from Australian acacias to Japanese cycads. The acacias, sometimes referred to as mimosas, were a favourite of Thomas's. By the end of 1867, only nine months after purchasing his garden, he had acquired 47 different species of acacia. Their vivid yellow flowers in the spring, with the blues of sea and sky, animate the gardens at La Mortola. *Acacia x hanburyana* is a particularly decorative example. A hybrid produced by Ludwig Winter and named in honour of Thomas, its compact habit and delicate glaucous foliage provide year-round appeal.

In contrast, the Japanese cycad, *Cycas revoluta*, was introduced to the garden as a result of Thomas's visits to its native country. A shipment of these plants was dispatched to La Mortola from Japan at the end of 1871. They have since become familiar features of parks and gardens along the Riviera. *C. revoluta* resembles a stunted cross between a tree fern and a palm, growing to a height of about two metres, with a chunky, scarred trunk topped by a whorl of frond-like leaves. The cycad is a dwindling remnant of prehistory, its leathery leaves once the food of dinosaurs, its presence on Earth dating back to the Carboniferous Period, 350 million years ago. They are dioecious, having separate male and female plants. The male produces a large, upright cone from its crown, while the female produces a nest of rust-brown nut-like seeds at the centre of its whorl of leaves. Cycads have not only fed dinosaurs, but human beings too. Some species contain edible deposits of starchy material: the common name of *Cycas circinalis* is the sago palm.

At the eastern flank of the palazzo the path continues its downward journey, but there are two possible change of direction. To the left runs the handsome pergola, or the Topia, as it is known at La Mortola; to the right is the arched gateway into the north terrace of the Palazzo Orengo. The Topia, shaded by climbing plants, curves gently across the garden to its eastern boundary, overlooking the Bay of Latte and across to Ventimiglia. Two thirds of the way along the Topia it is bisected by a flight of steps that travel, via pools and fountains, down into the Australian Wood of eucalyptus, melaleuca and brachychiton.

The palazzo is a building of informal grace and understated in its style. The solid bulk reflects its past as a fortified villa built around a well. The well is now an ornamental feature in the palazzo's hallway. Water, both source and ownership, has always been central to life at La Mortola. The solidity of the terracotta-washed walls is softened by the extensions and white marble embellishments of Thomas's programme of renovation. It took nine years to complete. The interior is smaller than one would expect; there are no endless corridors of salons. In its spare and lofty rooms the decoration that remains is calm and sophisticated. The evident craftsmanship in construction and finish is complemented by artful frescoes. The architectural style adopted by Thomas and his architect, Arthur Foster, was to be copied on the Riviera for more than 50 years. A fine example of these additions is the south front of the palazzo, where a beautiful loggia supported by barley-twist marble columns overlooks the sea and the rest of the garden. The palazzo is not the final destination of the pathway, but it is the punctuation mark in the garden's movement to the sea. From the gateway on Corso Monte Carlo both the eye and the body are drawn down to the sea.

From the southern terrace it is possible to follow a set of stairs that lead past the little formal gardens, which skirt the palazzo. Here, at the top of an avenue of funereal cypress, is an ornate pavilion known as the Moorish Kiosk or simply the *Mausoleo*, the mausoleum. This is the resting place of the ashes of Thomas Hanbury. At the bottom of the cypress avenue is the bridge over Via Aurelia, a Roman road. The avenue follows the sloping contours of the garden, marking the limits of the Australian Wood on one side, while on the other are the beginnings of the citrus collection. Beyond the fruit trees is the old tennis court, laid out by Thomas for his children. La Mortola was a family botanic garden. At the Strada romana all the footpaths, alleys, tracks and walks that have made their way down the hillside garden merge into one.

The Roman road is another memorial to the long and historic human influence that has shaped the Riviera. It cuts east to west right through the garden and parallel to the coast. It is inaccessible from within the grounds. The road surface of the Strada romana is deeply entrenched and well below the level of the garden above. It is traversed by a single footbridge, under which it has carved its unwavering course, like a dry canal. To the side of this bridge Thomas Hanbury erected a plaque, commemorating those who have passed along this ancient road, from popes to emperors, from Machiavelli to Napoleon Bonaparte. Today it is a little-used footpath and those who travel on it are less keen to have their journeys documented.

Over the bridge and down the stone steps on the other side the ground finally flattens out. This last portion of the garden is a flat spit of land that ends at the sea wall. It has provided man with one of the rare pieces of easily cultivated ground around La Mortola for thousands of years. When Thomas arrived it was planted with vines, fruit trees and vegetables, and it remained the site of a kitchen garden, a citrus orchard and a vineyard. Those days have gone, however. There is still an orchard here, but the vines have been grubbed up and the vegetables have disappeared. The way from the bridge towards the sea is straight and lined with olive trees and ranks of citrus trees. The old and redundant olive press, which is positioned decoratively at the end of the path, makes for an eloquent statement on the inevitable change of the garden's function. Below the mill, or Tempietto del frantoio, is a small café, which caters for the garden's visitors. Behind it lie the sea and the beach where Thomas Hanbury first set foot on Capo Mortola. His first experience of La Mortola in the spring of 1867 was from the sea, as he arrived for a picnic from Menton.

Today, it is no longer possible to gain access to the gardens from the sea. The sturdy wall that sweeps along the coastal fringe of the garden has a couple of gateways, but these are chained and padlocked. For those with keys, however, the walk up through the garden from the pebble beach makes a diverting and effective alternative entrance to the garden. If the olive and cypress are the thematic leads at the top of the garden, then it is the pine that dominates the garden at its closest to the sea. Thomas planted a selection of pines at the edge of his property, most particularly *Pinus pinaster* and *P. maritima*. On the level projection of land that forms the actual cape of La Mortola these tough and elegant trees provide the first indication of a rocky shore becoming land. On the beach over which they tower the resinous perfume of the pines and their litter of pungent needles hangs heavy. It is a warm and comforting fragrance. As one looks around and grows accustomed to the beauty, a human response, perhaps, is to wonder less at the plants and more at the man who put them here. However, it is not by the sea, the site of Thomas Hanbury's initial and heady introduction to La Mortola, that a clue to the beginnings of the garden's personal narrative is to be found.

The stone gateway through which all visitors enter the garden carries upon it the first intimation of the human story behind the garden. Its outer wall carries the coat of arms of the Hanbury family, dating back to the 17th century. However, for a more poignant clue to the story of the man who founded the garden here, one must walk through the arched entrance. On the garden side of the portal is the keystone. Many are the visitors who pass through the gateway into the gardens at La Mortola but fail to spot the inscription above them of the Chinese character 'Fo'. Of those who do most would be unaware of its significance. In 1879 a gentleman from China named Kuo Sung Tao visited Thomas at La Mortola, staying for a few days en route to Naples. On his departure he presented Thomas with the inscription: its meaning is 'Happiness'. Kuo Sung Tao was the first Chinese ambassador ever to be sent to the West by that great imperial power. The embassy marked a profound moment in China's fraught relations with Britain, reflecting the ebbing powers of the Manchu Dynasty. The visit of Kuo Sung Tao to this tiny coastal village is not only testament to the standing of Thomas Hanbury within China, but also gives some indication of the importance of China to Thomas and, by extension, to the garden and its environs.

The wealth that Thomas brought to Capo Mortola had been made in Shanghai. Whatever Thomas's achievements were in Italy, they were intrinsically linked to, and paid for by, his labours in China. As for Thomas Hanbury the man, of all the papers and letters that he left it is those relating to China that reveal the most about him and the moral complexities of the world he inhabited. He was to live for almost 75 years, 15 of which he spent in Shanghai. The years in China proved to be the most formative of his life.

# Chapter Two
# Shanghai bound

On 4 July 1853 the 21-year-old Thomas Hanbury stepped on board *Bengal*, a ship of the P&O line, at Southampton, bade farewell to his parents and his uncle, and set sail for Shanghai. With the £6,000 that his father, Daniel Bell Hanbury, had lent him, Thomas had gone into partnership with his cousin and three others. They hoped to make their fortunes in the city on the delta of the mighty Yangtze, with its flotillas of vessels carrying tea and silk to the rest of the world. Four years earlier Thomas had ended his formal education and started working for a City of London tea brokers, William James Thompson & Sons of Mincing Lane. His apprenticeship had not only left him with knowledge of the tea trade and bookkeeping, it had nurtured the nascent business acumen and ambition that possessed him.

China had been chosen as the arena for Thomas's pursuit of wealth for some very specific reasons. By 1853, after centuries of self-imposed isolation had ended, China's vast resources and markets had finally been exposed to the glare of European and American capitalism. The waning imperial power of the Manchu (or Ching) Dynasty had struggled to stem the irresistible mercantile tide of the West. Torpid with corruption and stultified by social turmoil, China was rich, vulnerable and unstable. By the middle of the 19th century the Manchu Dynasty, whose emperors had been absolute rulers of China since 1661, was beginning to crumble. Thomas was an astute, determined and skilful entrepreneur, but the foundation of his enormous wealth was the political and economic climate of 19th-century China. Without some understanding of the China that Thomas was sailing towards in 1853 any comprehension of this deeply significant period of Thomas's life would be less than complete.

Since the 16th century imperial China had failed to demonstrate an enthusiasm for international trade equal to that of the European maritime empires. In 1521 China gave up overseas trade, and committed itself to cultural and economic purdah. The empire was largely self-sufficient and most Europeans who had visited it had shown themselves to belong to a civilization so inferior to China's that they were clearly little more than barbarians. Consequently any discourse with them was not only unnecessary but also dishonourable. This disdain for all things European was still prevalent into the late 19th century. Such was the public disgrace of dealing with the West that Chinese civil servants were known to break down and weep when informed of their 'promotion' to the Chinese equivalent of the Foreign Office, the Tsungli Yamen. The common term for Europeans among the Chinese at that time was '*fan kuei*', or 'foreign devils'. The trade that continued was done under sufferance and at arm's length. The Portuguese were tolerated, but they were confined to Macao. During the Ming and the Manchu Dynasties, up until the early 19th century, the only Europeans to penetrate China further than the docks of a handful of ports were Catholic missionaries. This did not prevent merchants from sailing to China, nor did it prevent the growth of trade. The British, French and Dutch were quick to emulate the Portuguese. The markets of Europe were greedy, even if the conditions were difficult for their traders. Chinese silk was much sought after by merchants, but for the British there was one product of China that commanded their interest above all others: tea.

The British obsession with tea had begun more than 200 years before Thomas began to learn the rudiments of business practice in a London tea brokers. The first commercial shipment of China tea had arrived in London in 1652. By 1660 tea was fashionable enough for Samuel Pepys to remark on 'tee, a china drink', and by 1686 the British East India Company had pretty much cornered the market in the tea trade between China and Britain. It was a lucrative monopoly, which the Company enjoyed until 1834. The Company made a profit of £100 on every ton of tea imported into Britain during the 18th century. By 1801 an average of two and a half pounds of tea leaves was being used by every man and woman in England every year. In 1820 30 million pounds of tea were shipped to Britain for consumption by its inhabitants. Tea was an enormously valuable commodity for the British East India Company and China was its only source.[1]

By the end of the 18th century the only port open for trade with the barbarian nations was Canton (Guangzhou). Since 1720 a complex and infuriating method of trading had been imposed on the Europeans. It was called the *Co-hong* system, referring to the officially sanctioned Chinese merchants through whom the Europeans were forced to do business. It was a deeply corrupt system, because of the total lack of fixed tariffs and the abundant avarice of the Co-hong. The foreign merchants were barred from any form of official contact and they were subject to Chinese laws. For the foreigners there was precious little equality in the courts. Any legal argument or business transaction was made doubly fraught by the complete ban on any Chinese subject teaching their language to a foreigner. Attempts to encourage the Chinese to adopt a more satisfactory system for the merchants had been made by the British. In 1793 Lord Macartney led a delegation, which achieved little, while the mission headed by Lord Amherst in 1816 served only to exacerbate the diplomatic problems.

Trade with China was complicated by another factor. The vastness and diversity of China's lands and peoples, coupled with its ancient and sophisticated culture, meant that China had little interest in anything that the West had to offer. China did very much more selling than it did buying. As mentioned above, China was self-sufficient and this created a problem for the barbarians. At its most basic, the trading nations came to Canton with the only goods that excited the Chinese: gold, copper and, most importantly, silver. They left with tea, silk, cotton and heaps of porcelain to serve as valuable ballast on their ships. China swallowed up the silver. The traders returned with more silver and so the process was repeated, time and time again. Silver, wealth in its crudest, shiniest, most glorious form, was flowing out of the West and into the great ocean of China. China bought nothing from the foreign traders and this did not represent a balance of trade. The West desperately needed a commodity that was cheap to produce, that would have an inexhaustible appeal and that the Chinese would be prepared to pay for in silver.

Man's use of opium, both as a medicine and as a narcotic, has a long history. At a prehistoric burial sight in southern Spain some dried seed capsules were found amid the dust. These capsules were from *Papaver somniferum*, the opium poppy, and have been dated to around 4200 BC. Their presence was certainly not coincidental. It is believed that the cultivation of the opium poppy, as opposed to the harvesting of wild material, can be traced back to at least 3400 BC, in the locality of the Tigris and the Euphrates (modern Iraq). At Deir el-Medina in Egypt a small pot was removed from inside the tomb of Kha, containing 3,000-year-old opium. The Chinese had made use of opium and its properties for centuries, long before their first contact with the ruthless traders of the West, having probably been introduced to it through trade with the Middle East. By 1729 the problems of addiction associated with opium use were increasingly evident to the imperial government. The Manchus declared opium illegal. Opium continued to be used recreationally, however, by the indolent wealthy. It was a luxury item, supplied mostly by the Portuguese.[2]

A new market leader, however, was in the making. In June 1757 Robert Clive, at the head of a force of 3,200 Indian and European troops, cunningly defeated an army of an estimated 68,000 under the command of Suraj-ud-Dowlah at the Battle of Plassey. The effect of this battle was to confirm Britain's supremacy in India. Plassey was written into the canon of the great victories of the British Empire. A less celebrated effect of Clive's triumph was to free up some of the best agricultural land in India, land ripe for exploitation by the East India Company. By 1758 the Company had secured the monopoly for opium production in India and the sowing of new lands with poppies had begun. Indian opium became the magic commodity, the silver bullet that would balance trade in Canton. In 1774 Clive died from an overdose of opium, a drug that he had taken to treat a bowel complaint and to which he had become addicted.

By 1773 the British had replaced the Portuguese as the leading opium dealers and by 1776 they were bringing more than 60 tons a year into China from India. By 1830 this figure had more than doubled, to 150 tons. The estimate that there were some 12 million opium smokers in China by the end of the 1830s gives an idea of the scale and value of the market to the dealers and traders.

Since the importation of opium into China was still forbidden by law the Chinese complained to the British government, but British officials denied any responsibility for the actions of a private company. The East India Company itself was equally elusive: it was sorry, but it really had no control over the matter. All the opium that it produced was auctioned by the Company in Calcutta. It could hardly be blamed for what occurred after the product had been sold. Many of the Chinese officials were happy to collaborate with the British and, increasingly, American opium smugglers, in such a manner that the trade flowed freely. A mixture of corruption and intimidation served the opium merchants well. Firms such as Jardine & Matheson dispatched well-armed ships, loaded with opium, to seek out addict-free *terra nova* along the Chinese coast, in order to expand the market. It is easy to see why the Chinese were more than a little mistrustful of these foreigners.

After 1834 the East India Company no longer enjoyed its monopoly of trade with China. The way was now open for any British firm to set up business, prepared though it must be for the still intransigent attitude of the Chinese government towards foreign traders. Lord Napier had come to China in 1834 in another attempt by the British to establish an even mercantile playing field. The mission was not a success, and the cultural impasse between the British and Chinese governments remained. China wanted an end to the illegal importation of opium and Britain wanted greater licence for its merchants. In 1839 20,291 chests of opium were destroyed by Chinese officials in Canton, an act that formed the catalyst for the First Opium War between Britain and China. The conflict was brought to a close by the defeat of the Manchu forces and the signing of the Treaty of Nanking in August 1842. This treaty was not just an admission of defeat; it was a statement of humiliation. The imperial government was to pay compensation of 21 million silver dollars to the British. This equates, approximately, to 70 million US dollars in today's currency. In addition, the Chinese were to cede Hong Kong, and the ports of Canton, Amoy, Foochow, Ningpo and Shanghai were to become open ports. Any foreign merchants within any of these ports were to enjoy rights of extraterritoriality. This meant that, although these merchants were resident and trading in China, they were outside the jurisdiction of Chinese law. They were beholden to the laws of their home nations instead. The prising open of the Chinese oyster had begun in earnest and it was clear that within its vast, once impenetrable shell lay rather more than just a single pearl. With the Treaty of Nanking and the new accessibility of those five ports, China became a beacon to men like Thomas Hanbury.

'I am favourably impressed with Shanghai on the whole, though to speak the truth, it is but a swamp':[3] the youthful Thomas Hanbury's first impression of Shanghai is accurate enough, for marshy it was, but Shanghai was a great deal more than poorly drained land. By 1853 Shanghai was the mercantile faucet through which flowed much of the worldly goods and personages that were carried on the River Yangtze. Thousands of years of depositing silt had contributed to making Shanghai the swamp it was, but the process had also created one of China's most fertile areas. The economy was one of cotton, silk and rice, but the river brought with it goods from a far larger area than just the environs of Shanghai. The landmass drained by the

Yangtze covers a territory equivalent in size to 80 per cent of Europe. Not surprisingly, in this huge region dominated by the third largest river in the world road was not the chosen medium of transport. The vein-like network of canals, tributaries, lakes and rivers all feeding in to the great artery of the Yangtze made a road system unnecessary. Almost everything and everyone travelled on the water.

The sophistication and the great age of Chinese culture are evident in the history of Shanghai and the districts that surround it. Shanghai began to make its mark on the area as the Yangtze silted up rival ports. The *North China Daily News* noted in its special publication for the Shanghai Jubilee in 1893 that: 'some 35 years after the Norman Conquest of England the Custom House was removed to Shanghai'. The locality was a magnet for enterprise and expansion. The city of Hangzhou, the capital of the Song Dynasty to the south of Shanghai, had, by the end of the 12th century, a population of more than 1 million, while the largest European city of that period registered a lowly 50,000 souls. By 1842 Shanghai had a population of about 400,000. The economic whirlwind of the next 60 years took the population to just short of 1 million.

The venerable city of Shanghai, its walls constructed in 1570, was not to be Thomas's home. The Treaty of Nanking compelled China to provide land for the traders, but it did not stipulate where. Within the walled city of Shanghai there was simply not the room, nor did the Chinese feel at all inclined to live too intimately with the *fan kuei*, the foreign devils, if it could be avoided. The land provided was in the marshy ground around the walls, supporting a separate settlement each for the French, the Americans and the British. At the time of Thomas's arrival the British Settlement occupied less than 150 acres, but the lack of clearly defined boundaries meant that dealers in real estate spent most of the next 100 years annexing new parcels of land. This arrangement provided the foreign nations with both power and freedom within China. In 1863 the American and British settlements were merged to form the International Settlement, administrated by the Shanghai Municipal Council, which had itself come into existence in 1854. Thus was the power of this 'republic dropped down on an alien empire' [4] consolidated.

In September 1853, as Thomas first gazed at the ancient walled city of Shanghai, or the 'Chinese City' as it known to foreigners, he was most perturbed by what he witnessed. Thomas had known that the city was not under any direct European or American influence, but the shock lay in the fact that neither was it under the control of the imperial government. The Chinese City was held by a band of rebels called the Small Knife Society and was under siege by the imperial forces. China was not only suffering from the external threat of the gunboat capitalists of Europe and the United States, but was also in a state of violent revolution from within.

The Manchus were not Chinese, but invaders whose roots lay in Manchuria, a province bordering what is now North Korea. Their ascent to the imperial throne had been achieved by a mixture of military skill and political opportunism. The centuries that followed saw some assimilation between Chinese and Manchu, but in essence it was a rule of subjugation. For example, while one's perception of the 'Chinaman' of days gone by is characterized by his shaven forehead and his queue, or pigtail, this coiffure was not dictated by fashion but was imposed by the victorious Manchu as a symbol of the submission of the vanquished Chinese. Since the 17th century the men of China had worn their hair as a mark of national prostration. Hair was a political issue and the rebels of the mid-19th century grew their hair long as a symbol of their rejection of the Manchu yoke.

From the very start of the dynastic reign of the Manchus, in the late 17th century, many Chinese had sought to rid their nation of these oppressors. Resistance to the Manchus took the form of secret societies, such as the innocuously named White Lily Society or the White Feather Society. The Manchu reprisals for the latter's failed attack on an imperial palace in 1813 saw the execution of more than 20,000 alleged members of the Society. However, the most influential of all the secret societies that riddled China were unquestionably the infamous Triads. Still prevalent in much organized crime today and enormously powerful, the Triads, known collectively as the Heaven and Earth Society, were born in the late 1600s out of the struggle against Manchu domination. The sole aim of the Triads at that time was to bring down the Manchu Dynasty. These conspiratorial societies and their machinations against the imperial regime became increasingly active from the 1790s.

The impoverished majority of the ever-increasing Chinese population was finding life a harder and harder struggle. In 1741 the population of China had been around 150 million. By the time that Thomas Hanbury arrived in 1853 the population had nearly tripled, to more than 435 million. The land belonged to the rich minority; the production of food was still at mid-18th-century levels. Corruption so infested the bureaucracy that taxes rose to levels beyond the means of millions of the poorest. The defeat of China by the British had made the economic plight of the Chinese worse still. It had also demonstrated the weakness and fallibility of the Manchu Dynasty to those who were desperate to overthrow it. Thus, by the 1850s China's political and social landscape provided fertile ground for popular insurrection.

In 1854 there were five separate rebellions taking place in China, led by the Taiping, the Red Turban, the Miao, the Nien and the Small Knife Society. The Small Knife Society sprang up in Fukien in May 1853, an offshoot of the ubiquitous Triads. It was a short-lived and small-scale movement compared to the others, and its control of Shanghai ended in 1855. The flags it flew from the ramparts of Shanghai were not exclusively in the colours of the Triads, however. The other flag on display was that of the Taiping. The Taiping had begun life as a small Christian group, the Society of God-Worshippers. It had been founded in 1846 by Hung Hsiu-ch'uan, a failed scholar and civil servant. The visions he had experienced, subsequent to reading some Protestant missionary tracts, inspired him to found a movement that almost destroyed the Manchus. The Taiping Rebellion had begun in earnest in 1851 and was finally brought to a close in 1866. During that time China endured a period of national cataclysm. Accurate figures are impossible to calculate but the enormity of this imprecision serves merely to underline the horror of the Taipeng Rebellion, as Ian Heath cites:

> even by conservative estimates 20–30 million people are believed to have died, a total only exceeded by the bloodiest conflict in history, the Second World War.[5]

It was the great military advances made by the Taiping that had provided the inspiration and confidence for such groups as the Small Knife Society to break into open revolt. The capture of Nanking by the Taiping in March 1853 was of huge psychological and strategic value to the rebels. The Taiping already held the Yangtze from Wuchang to Nanking: now they had control of the Grand Canal that linked the Yangtze Basin to the Manchu capital, Peking (or Beijing).

Shanghai presented itself as the last key city on the Yangtze remaining outside Taiping control. The Small Knife Society was ejected from Shanghai in February 1855, but the potential for a rebel assault on the city and its inhabitants remained. To secure Shanghai would be to have possession of the Yangtze, the main circuit cable of China.

Shanghai and its foreign settlements, due to their geographical and economic importance, spent the next 10 years under the fluctuating threat of attack from the Taiping. The destabilizing influence that this had on all elements of Shanghai's native and foreign communities was profound. For those foreigners in business, like Thomas Hanbury, the opportunities both to win and to lose great fortunes were clear. In that long period of most dreadful suffering, while markets surged and markets tumbled, the chances to demonstrate a dexterous and rewarding use of capital were many. More frequent still were the opportunities for charity and compassion.

# Chapter Three
## Topside Galah

The China that greeted Thomas Hanbury in 1853 was a nation beset by furious and bloody upheaval. In contrast, Thomas's background was one of domestic and professional regularity and industry.

Thomas was born in 1832, the fourth child and third son of Daniel Bell and Rachel Hanbury. The Hanburys were of ancient Quaker lineage, tracing their membership of the Society of Friends back to the time of George Fox and the birth of the Quaker movement in the revolutionary England of the mid-17th century. The Hanburys' faith was strong, and the Quaker principles of truth, honesty, charity and hard work formed the enduring core of Thomas's character. Another characteristic often associated with Quakers was also a crucial constituent of Thomas's personality: the rigorous and successful pursuit of financial gain.

The family home was in Bedford Lane in Clapham. Clapham was then a leafy village outside London and home to some of London's wealthier inhabitants seeking an escape from the grimy clamour of the city. Thomas's father, Daniel Bell Hanbury, was a partner in a successful and respected pharmaceutical company, Allen, Hanbury and Barry of Plough Court, Lombard Street, in the City of London. The family was financially comfortable and Thomas was educated at a Quaker school in Croydon, where the precepts of his Christian faith were firmly embedded in him.

The alien and extraordinary nature of Shanghai and its settlements must have proved exciting and stimulating to Thomas as he stepped ashore on 18 September 1853, but it must also have been confusing, if not a little disturbing. Some of the culture shock of his arrival may have been dissipated by the visits to Cairo, Aden (now in Yemen), Ceylon (now Sri Lanka) and Singapore that he had made as he had sailed to China. Yet this was the mid-19th century, a world without all the visual media that enclose, shrink and homogenize our planet and our cultures. Thomas was a 21-year-old Victorian bookkeeper. Until he boarded the steamer in Southampton the closest he had come to the 'mysteries of the Orient' had been a few weeks in Europe and visits to the Great Exhibition of 1851. Now he was thousands of miles and 72 days' sailing away from the only home he had known. There were no telephones and no telegrams. A letter could take months to arrive. Shanghai's great port was a frontier town in another world, a city that crossed enormous cultural boundaries. Yet even in Shanghai, for all its otherworldliness, the British Empire was never that far away. Thomas could enjoy potted shrimps and a game of cricket after work. In this confusing and contradictory city Thomas could chat merrily to a compatriot about the merits of the off-break, pausing only to allow the deafening roar of an explosion to die down as the siege guns blazed away at the old city's walls. Shanghai, let us not forget, was also a battlefield.

Shanghai sits on the edge of the huge Yangtze Delta, at the junction of two tributaries, the Whangpo and the Woosung, and is surrounded by silty marshland. Thomas describes the area in a letter dated 13 August 1854:

the countryside is perfectly flat, not the slightest elevation to be seen in any direction, it is one dead level of rich alluvial soil, intersected by numerous rivers, canals and creeks. Both cotton and rice are very extensively cultivated. The most remarkable feature of the country is the immense number of graves scattered in every direction. The Chinese here do not bury their dead under the ground as it is too swampy, but leave the bare coffins about the fields, for a year or two and then raise a mound of earth over them, of course they have the greatest respect for these mounds, and as they are never removed, and the population so large, the country is one succession of them. Nobody could believe the number unless they saw them … The settlement is a very small one as yet, only about 250 or 300 foreigners, who are all of the better class, that is merchants or their assistants, in fact we are all rich, or getting rich in China, no poor people, the houses from a distance, coming up the river, for instance look almost like a collection of palaces. They are all stuccoed white and the walls about the settlement are also white so that it is dazzling, and injurious to the eyes to walk about when the sun is shining, the Chinese city is about half a mile distant.

The eerie landscape provided a most enigmatic backdrop to the events that dominate Thomas's early letters, written during the siege of Shanghai. The Small Knife Society had captured the city shortly before Thomas's arrival and was now being besieged by between 12,000 and 13,000 troops of the Chinese imperial Army. The neutral foreign settlements, situated outside the city walls, were constantly on the fringe of the skirmishes and battles that punctuated the siege. Shanghai's walls may have been half a mile away, but the suburbs of the Chinese City spread out to the edge of the settlements. Often the Europeans would find themselves in the middle of a battle, with cannon balls passing overhead. Occasionally buildings would be damaged: Thomas was most excited one day to find that a cannon-ball had buried itself in his garden path. With the Taiping holding Nanking further upriver, the time of year and the state of affairs in Shanghai, business slowed to a standstill. Thomas had a great deal of time to observe the absurdities and the tragedies of this erratic conflict, and its effects on both the Chinese and the foreign contingent of which he was a member. His descriptions and thoughts are most revealing, illuminating his character, his strength, humour and compassion. He is a witness with an opinion, never afraid of voicing his disgust at cruelty and inhumanity, whether Chinese or British.

Many elements of the siege appeared risible to Thomas. In a letter written on 22 October 1853, after a month of watching the daily mêlées, he writes simply of the battle: 'it is a complete farce'. A passage describes how a shortage of cannon-balls on both sides:

> is realised by native boys, who with strong commercial instincts place themselves in sheltered positions between combatants. Marking where a ball buries itself in the soft earth, they rush out to the spot, dig it out and with complete impartiality sell the projectile to whichever side offers the better price.

The fighting was often more for display than for destruction, with so much noise and thunder, to so little effect, that Thomas remarks that 'the quantity of gunpowder to kill a man must be very great'.[1]

The rebels in the Small Knife Society were never acknowledged as allies by the Taiping, much to their dismay, nor did the Europeans offer the support that had been hoped for. The rebels were a 'tatterdemalion' bunch and 'land pirates', as Thomas describes them, made up of a curious mélange of villains, adventurers and mercenaries of bizarre provenance. The following excerpt from a letter written by Thomas to his mother in February 1854 is most instructive. The peculiar relationship between the Europeans and the rebels is clearly illustrated, but there is also evidence of Thomas's observant sense of the ridiculous. It is indicative, too, of his warm relationship with his mother and their shared sense of humour. Thomas writes of the Small Knife Society:

> they are extremely gaudy in appearance wearing splendid silks of all colours but principally red … the third in command used to be house boy to a gentleman of the name of Skinner and still goes by the name of Skinners house boy, though his real name is Lin. On China new years day a party comprising his old master went into the city to see him, he received them quite in state, and treated them to a Champagne lunch with potted anchovies and other European delicacies. It is principally by such characters as this that the city is held.
>
> A great many have been connected with foreigners in some way – thus for instance one of their chief men was formerly James Crampton's valet and was discharged by him for stealing a silver spoon, then there are about 15 sailors, who I believe point their cannon for them and to crown all an American surgeon, a sad drunken fellow, who often heads their sallies, sometimes in a state of intoxication holding a sword in each hand.
>
> The other morning we were all much startled by the most horrendous report which shook the houses, like an earthquake. This was a mine that the Imperialists had excavated in a very clever manner, and almost unknown to the other party, the explosion was so great that six panes of glass were broken in Dr Lockhart's house, while a large gap was made in the walls, upon this some desperate fighting ensued, but the rebels headed by the drunken

doctor and Skinners house boy sallied out and drove the assailants back with great slaughter, the latter receiving a bullet in the shoulder which however does not prove a serious wound.

Thomas watched the engagements between the rebels and the imperial forces with a cool detachment, amused at times and appalled at others. His tone is mostly one of bemused neutrality as to what occurs between the Chinese. Less than two months earlier Thomas had reported that this happy band of rebels had found that supplies and money were running low. They had fallen into a dispute among themselves that grew into something altogether more serious. At its conclusion 179 of the rebels were dead.

Thomas reserved his deepest scorn for his own community, the foreigners. In November 1853 the imperial troops became aware that one of the foreign trading houses was shipping arms to the rebels. A detachment of some 400 Chinese soldiers entered the Settlement to intercept the cargo. Some British marines, who were on guard at the church and were startled at the sudden appearance of so many Chinese, had opened fire. The imperial troops had fled at once, but the marines and several civilians had blazed away with their assorted firearms at the backs of the fast-retreating Chinese. Three of the fleeing soldiers were killed. Thomas writes of his compatriots' behaviour:

this conduct I consider quite disgraceful, and indeed I think if people had not been precipitous all bloodshed would have been avoided for I think they had no idea of attacking us, for the officer commanding them politely alighted from his horse, and came to explain the reason of their coming to the officers on duty at the church, who however, could not understand Chinese. The fact is that there is such a thirsting for blood among the English and Americans…[2]

Thomas was understandably fascinated by the siege that played itself out around the Settlement like a grand piece of theatre. It dominated the lives of all the inhabitants of the Settlement. The viewing and discussing of the constant skirmishes provided one of the few genuinely diverting alternatives to the regular tedium of the small foreign community. Surrounded by the clash of battle, frustrated by watching what was perceived to be a cowardly impasse between the two Chinese armies and feeling increasingly threatened by the imperial troops, the young men of the Settlement began to arm themselves. A militia was formed, called the Shanghai Volunteers. Thomas's Quaker beliefs were at odds with the increasingly belligerent tones of his friends and colleagues. In a letter to his mother dated 28 November 1853 he writes:

Some gentleman called the other day to ask us to belong to the volunteer corps, and afterwards sent round a paper with a request that we would fill in the amount of arms we wanted out from England. I sent it back with the name of our firm and written against it 'none', as it was only T.C.jr [Thomas's cousin, Thomas Christy junior] who wanted any and I thought he had far better attend to his business than learn the way to destroy his fellow-creatures.

In April 1854, after imperial troops assaulted three members of the Settlement, injuring one badly, a joint force of American and British traders and marines attacked the imperial camp close by the Settlement. The imperial troops retreated swiftly and their camp was destroyed. In the chaotic advance two foreigners were killed and 15 injured, some by 'friendly fire'. The incident came to be known as the Battle of Muddy Flat and became a celebrated piece of Settlement history. One young man, G.G. Gray, who had accompanied Thomas on the voyage from England, was shot in the knee. The damage was so severe that his leg had to be amputated that evening. Yet Thomas had refused to fight.

For a young Englishman in 1854, surrounded by his peers, to refuse to take part in the defence, not only of his small community, but also of the honour of his country and that of the victims of the assaults, one of whom was a woman, was an act of remarkable strength of character and principle. Thomas held fast to the tenets of the Quaker faith. Thomas was thousands of miles away from home, with only his equally compromised cousin to report his behaviour. There was never any question of the imperial troops putting up strong resistance, so he could simply have gone along with everyone and never fired a shot. He chose instead to invite abuse, gossip, accusations of cowardice and potential ostracism by the tiny community of the Settlement, because he believed that it was wrong to kill another human being, European or Chinese. His sister Anna received a letter from him describing the 'battle' and containing this passage:

> I was the only one in our house who did not bear arms, and of course I was somewhat taunted in consequence... The former volunteer corps has been dissolved and they are now organising a new one, Mr Webb, Mrs Thompson's brother, was round at our office the day before yesterday trying very hard to induce us to join. I refused entirely, but I can assure thee I find it a difficult thing to withstand the importunities from friends in a small community like this, almost every one is expected to help, and I do feel it very much I assure thee when I see my friends go out

and risk their lives, for the protection of my property and life not that I care for any accusation of cowardice which I know would be untrue, but it is a difficult thing to know how to act.[3]

It was not only in his Quaker beliefs concerning violence toward his fellow human beings that Thomas stood out from his compatriots. Thomas differed from the majority of the British and other foreigners in Shanghai in that his attitude to the Chinese was open, appreciative and fair-minded, and his attitude to the aggression and excesses of the foreigners was critical. In his first month in Shanghai Thomas commented on the Chinese in a letter to his mother dated 28 November 1854:

> the greater part of the people here do not understand the Chinese at all and treat them ill, but it is the easiest thing in the world to gain their friendship and they are delighted with any little condescension shewn them by a foreigner.

Thomas quickly came to appreciate the value of good relations with the Chinese from the point of view of business, 'they have the greatest confidence in foreigners and will trust them for months with any amounts without security, provided they know them to be respectable'. This observation so early in Thomas's career in Shanghai proved vital in his swift accumulation of a vast fortune.

The great fog of language hid understanding of China and the Chinese from the consciousness of the foreigners. The incident by the church related above was caused by the British officers' inability to understand Chinese. By January 1854, however, Thomas had begun lessons in Mandarin Chinese. Few of the foreigners in the Settlement bothered to learn Chinese and those that did were almost all missionaries or officials of the Consulate or the Custom House. Each firm, or *hong*, employed a *compradore*, an English-speaking Chinese man, who mediated in the trade between the foreigners and his countrymen. Hanbury & Company's compradore was a man called Lai Sun, who had been educated in the United States and spoke English fluently. Such a skill was a valuable commodity in itself: the Small Knife Society offered to double his salary if he came to work for them as their official interpreter. The compradores were a vital link in the chain of trade and many of them amassed tidy fortunes before going into business for themselves.

The vast majority of communication between the foreign community and the Chinese was executed through the crude filter of Pidgin English. It is difficult to overestimate the importance of this barbarous tongue. Not only does pidgin reflect the poverty of relations between the two camps, it was often instrumental in forming and sustaining the insensitive, ignorant and unsophisticated perceptions that characterized East–West relations, in China as elsewhere. Any suggestion of even the simplest intellectual or emotional expression was bludgeoned from conversation by pidgin. In a lecture entitled 'China As I Knew It' that Thomas delivered years later in Italy, he makes it clear that the distaste and frustration that he felt for pidgin and its imposition had not diminished:

> the ordinary resident after five years knows no more of the Chinese language than he did on landing, he communicates with the natives by means of a ridiculous jargon which may be described as English baby-talk, interspersed with an occasional Portuguese or bastard Chinese word. To convey a small idea of this degrading language I will give you the well-known lines in 'Excelsior' done into pidgin English: –

'Topside Galah'
That nightee teem begin chop-chop,
One young man walkee, no can stop –
Maskee colo, maskee icee,
He cally that flag, wid chop so nicee,
'Topside Galah!'[4]

Since Thomas delivered his lecture Henry Longfellow's poem 'Excelsior' has slipped somewhat from the popular canon. The original verse reads:

The shades of night were falling fast
As through an Alpine village passed
A youth, who bore, 'mid snow and ice,
A banner with the strange device,
Excelsior!

Months after Thomas had arrived in China, it was still worthy of remark to hear Dr Medhurst, one of the British missionaries, speaking Chinese. Thomas ventured into the besieged city with Dr Medhurst, who twice weekly took in supplies of rice for the starving remnants of Shanghai's population. The city had been devastated by more than six months' bombardment, and only those reduced to begging, and the rebels, remained. The rice was distributed after a sermon:

not a few had come to hear the preaching which was all in Chinese, Dr M. having a perfect command of the language, which sounds a strange jargon to European ears, particularly in a sermon, it was a most curious sight I can assure thee to one unaccustomed to it.[5]

Thomas's presence distributing rice inside the war-torn Chinese City further illustrates the fact that he was not the usual foreign trader. His interest in botany and horticulture may equally well have set him apart from his contemporaries in Shanghai. Daniel Hanbury, his eldest brother, was a notable botanist and pharmacist, and had always encouraged in Thomas an interest in plants and horticulture. The years that Thomas spent in Shanghai saw a constant stream of correspondence between the two brothers. The letters are rather lighter on business than many of the others written by Thomas, but are predictably very much heavier on flora and fauna. A typical passage from one of Daniel's letters runs:

> Hwa-tseaou Tree is not a new species but is the *Zanthoxylon alatum* of Wallich as we proved by comparing The Hang-Chow specimens with a fine series of *Z. alatum* from Dr Hooker's *Indian Herbarium*. It is therefore a different plant from that figured by Kaempfer among his plants of Japan and which is called *Zanthoxylon piperitum*.[6]

The majority of the raw materials used by Daniel in his work *Notes on Chinese Materia Medica* came to him through the offices of Thomas, who sent him everything from wisteria seeds and rhubarb, to the skull of a sea leopard and a cup made from rhinoceros horn. The importance of this shared interest to Thomas must have been considerable as he struggled with the endless business, the social isolation and the tedium of Shanghai. His enthusiasm for collecting material for Daniel can be gauged by an unfortunate incident that had occurred even before Thomas's arrival in China. The ship had called in at Singapore and Daniel had requested that an item of interest be procured for him. So determined was Thomas to oblige his brother that he was late for the ship that was to have taken him on the next leg of his voyage. It sailed without him.

Thomas began his own garden in China as soon as he was able, planting it with oranges, camellias and magnolias, and proudly informing Daniel that: 'my garden has been raised at a cost of over twenty pounds'.[7] Daniel's opinion was sought on the subject of lawns. By the mid-1860s Thomas had taken to planting trees, at his own cost, in the public areas of the settlement. In particular, Thomas laid out the Bund, which still runs alongside the river and serves as a public promenade, with ginkgos and camphor trees. The Chusan palm, *Trachycarpus fortunei*, was another favourite in Thomas's municipal planting, its name containing a tribute to the celebrated plant collector Robert Fortune (see below). Thomas was also to plant this palm at La Mortola. When he returned to Shanghai in 1869, after an absence of more than three years, he continued his public tree planting. He had no intention of staying permanently in Shanghai: the trees he planted there would be for others to enjoy.

It was in Shanghai, through Daniel's connections, that Thomas began slowly to become attached to the botanic world. Thomas was a useful pair of eyes for friends of Daniel's such as William and Joseph Hooker, who from 1855 onwards formed a father-and-son team as Director and Assistant Director at the Royal Botanic Gardens, Kew. As China became increasingly accessible to foreign nations, organisations such as the RHS, botanic gardens and commercial nurseries commissioned botanists and horticulturalists, like Robert Fortune, to gather the floral wealth of China. Fortune had first come to China in 1842 and returned to Britain with such garden favourites as *Weigela florida* and *pom-pom cultivars* of Chrysanthemum for the RHS. Most significantly, Fortune was responsible for smuggling tea plants out of China and introducing them to India on behalf of the East India Company. It is quite possible that Fortune's first book, *Three Years'*

*Wanderings in the Northern provinces of China* (1847), may have contributed to the young Thomas's enthusiasm for China.

Thomas was keen to meet the famous Fortune, but found that Shanghai society was unimpressed by the great man. Thomas wrote to Daniel:

> most people run him down here, and say his last work is a made-up affair and greatly exaggerated, besides they affirm he did not write it himself, but merely collected the matter.[8]

In a letter dated 3 May 1857 Daniel expresses his disappointment at Fortune's efforts:

> Fortune is not considered a botanist at all. All that he has sent from China have been showy flowering things such as would please the Horticultural Society who sent him on his first journey to China.[9]

One botanist sent out to the Far East by Kew in order to collect specimens of more scientific interest was Charles Wilford. He proved somewhat unreliable. His methods of sending back letters and material were so erratic that Thomas was asked to investigate. It appears that the temptations of the Orient were too much for Mr Wilford. Thomas wrote on 18 August 1860 to Daniel: 'Wilford I fear is quite wild, I have been told as much by naval officers who have been with him in the same ship.'[10]

It was condemnation indeed, one would imagine, to be censured by naval officers on the grounds of immoral behaviour. Wilford was not alone in succumbing to the dissolute opportunities on offer in China. Thomas discovered early in his Shanghai career that rather too many of his fellow Europeans in the city proved worthy of the epithet 'foreign devils'.

# Chapter Four
## Foreign devils

The challenges of alien cultures for Thomas were not confined to dealings with the Chinese. It was not only the bellicose style of the other Europeans and the Americans with whom he now shared a strip of China that Thomas found uncomfortable. The great distance that lay between Shanghai and Clapham was not measured in miles alone. In a letter of 20 September 1853 Thomas tells his cousin Samuel Gurney that 'the houses here are truly magnificent and the people live in great luxury'. Each house was home to an individual firm or company and the terms 'house' and 'firm' were interchangeable. The home, its interior décor and its table were not simply accommodation and furnishings, but an exhibition of commercial success. A lavish dinner or soirée was less an evening's entertainment than an advertisement. The simple furniture that was shipped over for Thomas from dear old Bedford Lane was met with scorn by one old Shanghai hand, William Crampton:

> he says we must keep our position and that if we shewed such rubbish here we should be laughed at...almost everyone here has Canton furniture which is as magnificent as any I have ever seen.[1]

Appearances were all too important for the expatriate community, many spending all their earnings on the upkeep of their lavish lifestyles, in contrast to the Quaker ways that Thomas was used to. In Shanghai gratuitous extravagance, far from being frowned upon, was encouraged:

> our table is quite luxuriously spread, fresh fish every morning, besides eggs, bacon, mutton chops, beef steaks and generally a joint, at tiffin we have cold meat, pies, puddings, bread and cheeses with beer and wine, and at dinner soup, meat, game, pies, pudding, custards and fruits.[2]

In less than six months, despite frequent colds and inevitable moments of recalcitrant bowels, Thomas was describing himself as 'fat & flourishing'.[3] He had put on 10 pounds in weight since landing at Shanghai:

> More wine and beer are drunk than in England, everybody declaring it is impossible to get on in the climate without taking plenty; this did not suit my book at all and I have quite changed making tiffin my dinner and taking an old-fashioned tea when they take their dinner. I have also almost given up beer and wine which I do not think suit me well in this climate.[4]

It was not just the excessive eating and drinking that Thomas found unfamiliar:

> I have had many invitations to dinner lately, and as one cannot refuse them, it has become almost too much of a good thing; [Charles] Pullan and I were invited to one house lately where we sat for two or three hours in the dining room round an extremely hot fire, and every one in the room smoking but myself; the

atmosphere may be imagined, I felt as if I was suffocating and Pullan at last deadly pale that we had to bolt for the door, for fear he should faint, and the next morning we both got up with splitting headaches ... This abominable smoking is an intolerable nuisance I scarcely know how to bear it in the house of an evening ... the habit I am sorry to say has quite grown upon T.[homas] Christy.[5]

Thomas's detailing of his companions' habits and, most of all, those of his cousin, Thomas Christy, earned him the reputation within his partnership of being something of a sneak. His parents, despite Thomas's pleas, showed all his letters to his uncle, a backer of Hanbury & Company, and fussing father to Thomas Christy. Any hopes that his mother would conceal things from her own brother were misplaced. Understandably, Thomas Christy junior was unhappy with this lack of confidentiality, particularly as they were business partners. Thomas was reprimanded: 'I have been accused of trying to injure the interests of the firm and a thousand other things.'

Thomas, clearly, was not the typical European trader. He did not enjoy overindulgence. He neither relished drinking and smoking nor did he treat the Chinese with contempt. In fact in Thomas's letters he was critical of these habits in others. He had thus alienated his cousin, who might have been expected to be his one natural ally. All these factors would have served to marginalize him, even if his refusal to join the Shanghai volunteers had not marked him as beyond the social pale for many of his colleagues in the British Settlement.

Matters worsened following a major row at work between Thomas Hanbury and William Crampton in 1854. Hanbury & Company looked to trade in just about anything. On their arrival in Shanghai its staff dealt for the Rothschild family's bank, through the business

contacts of the anxious Uncle Thomas Christy. The firm made investments and loans, and traded currency, on behalf of the Rothschilds.
The backbone of the business, however, was in tea and silk. The division of labour was, according to Thomas: 'Pullans is tea taster, I keep
the books, my cousin (T. Christy jr) the godown.' The *godown* was
the company's warehouse. The members of the firm lived, worked,
dined and socialized together. It was an arrangement that could foster a powerful team spirit, but could equally degenerate into personal
bickering and soured relationships.

James and William Crampton were the other two partners in the
firm. The Cramptons were older than the others and had longer
experience of trading in China. Both these factors gave the
Cramptons considerable advantage over their partners, which
William exploited ruthlessly. Thomas was always complimentary
about James Crampton's skill in business and he clearly enjoyed his
company, despite James's reluctance to help with the daily administrative grind of the office. William Crampton was rather less
amenable than his brother, but was very capable of securing profitable deals for Hanbury & Company. His manner towards the
younger partners was high-handed, aggressive and dismissive.
Thomas and William Crampton did not get on, and tensions within
the company became increasingly evident. Then the inevitable row
occurred. The incident damaged the partnership irrevocably, but it
seems to have been a partnership that was ill-fated from its start.

Not long after the row William Crampton returned to England for
several months. Thomas remained to run the office, effectively single-
handed, since James Crampton declined to help him, young Thomas
Christy was proving useless and Charles Pullan, the tea-taster, was
debilitated by dysentery. After Pullan was finally sent home as a result

of his illness, William Crampton apparently wrote to his brother: 'I am sorry for poor Pullen, and I only wish it had been that — — Hanbury instead.' This was an exhausting period for Thomas, but one that bolstered his confidence and his reliance on his own abilities.

William Crampton, meanwhile, had visited the Hanbury family in Clapham. The cooler air of England had done nothing to dissipate his rancour. He made several allusions to Thomas's inability to keep the books accurately, his disagreeable nature and his refusal to socialize with the other members of the Settlement. All these traits, Crampton claimed, were jeopardizing Hanbury & Company's potential for profit. In a concerned letter that arrived in Shanghai on 28 January 1855, Thomas's mother referred to the criticisms made by Crampton. The accusations and the anxious tone of the letter came as a welcome excuse for Thomas to reveal his true feelings: his reply was sent the same day. In righteous indignation he defended himself robustly, spurred on by the suspicion that his parents might have been taken in by Crampton. Thomas informed his parents that Crampton was 'the most violent and passionate man I have ever lived with', and that he had 'not the slightest control of his temper'. Having begun with Crampton the individual, he warms to his theme and goes on to rail against the moral corruption of the Settlement as a whole. The reason for his apparent aloofness from the rest of the community is not arrogance, he explains, but profound distaste for what it represents. The dinners are little better than orchestrated gluttony, displays of gross overindulgence in food, alcohol, tobacco, indecency and gambling. The dinners simply reflect the professional standards of most of those who enjoy them, men for whom business involves illegality, defrauding the Custom House and cheating the Chinese:

the motto of every one seems to be 'Get dollars in the quickest way you can without reference to the means.' There is certainly not a strict, upright and honest firm in the place according to my ideas. Of course, a person coming from England is much disgusted with all this and I confess I perhaps was more so than other folks – Well I know I am often obstinate and I refused to fall into the ways of those around me...

As early as 18 August 1854 the tedium and the absence of like-minded spirits began to depress Thomas. In a letter to a family friend he writes:

I cannot say that I am particularly happy here; away from all my friends, Shanghai is a dull place, the country perfectly level and not particularly interesting, then the society's miserable, scarcely any ladies that are really worthy of the name. I but rarely visit and hardly ever go out to dinner or to parties; everyone here seems intent on getting money...

This was a complaint that appears with some regularity in Thomas's letters from Shanghai, for many years to come. The unclubbable Thomas was already set apart from many of his European and American colleagues; there were too many of the same ilk as Crampton, both men and women. The Settlement may have had a small population, but it was always big on parties, parties that Thomas chose to avoid and to which he was no longer invited. The letters that he wrote during the first year and a half of his life in Shanghai establish very clearly the nature of the man. Thomas was still only in his early twenties, but his indomitable strength of character was not to be compromised.

The dissatisfaction he expressed at the height of the Crampton crisis never disappeared. In 1857 the previous partnership was dissolved, and Hanbury & Company became Bower, Hanbury & Company. Thomas went back to Britain for a rest and a holiday. On his return to Shanghai the frenzy of commerce began once more. The contractual obligations of the partnership meant that the earliest that Thomas could quit Shanghai was 1865. His new partner Frederick Bower was capable of enormous industry and Thomas's carrying of the old firm had habituated him to working long hours. His social engagements were few: 'As usual I have little to say. Our existence here is comprised in two words, buying and selling, or perhaps one might add, making figures, eating, drinking and sleeping.'[6] Melancholy and loneliness welled up through the mesh of percentages, investments and silk prices that structured both his correspondence and his waking hours. In a letter to his brother Daniel, written on 19 March 1860, the strain is beginning to tell:

It is difficult to describe to you how my nervous system is not as strong as in England... I feel I am always inclined to take a gloomy view of any subject. Such an event as the arrival of the mail causes me to tremble, hands to shake and voice to fail more or less. A little cheerful society does me the world of good but I hardly ever get that.[7]

The siege of Shanghai and, with it, the existence of the Small Knife Society, ended in February 1855. The imperial troops required the assistance of French firepower to eject the shabby mob that had occupied the city since before Thomas's arrival, in September 1853. The social and political instability was not to diminish, however, but increased. The Small Knife Society had never been anything more than a sideshow to the main event, the Taiping Rebellion. This vast and devastating upheaval threw the whole of China into chaos and uncertainty, but Shanghai in particular languished under its shadowy threat until 1864.

However, Shanghai and its foreign settlements went on expanding, not just in spite of the rebellion, but because of it. The Small Knife Society's anarchic occupation of old Shanghai had brought a flood of Chinese refugees to the foreign settlements. As a result of the extraterritoriality secured after the First Opium War, the settlements were viewed as a safe haven by Chinese and the security provided by the foreigners was worth paying for. The influence this had on property prices was enormous. From Thomas's earliest days in China he had realized that land and housing had a profit potential unimaginable in England: 'the commonest place is now snapped up at an extravagant rent by Chinamen, who are glad to pay well, so that they can get into a place of safety.'[8]

In a letter written to his father in November 1853 Thomas illustrates the swift returns on property investment: Shaw, Bland & Company, he reports, owned a warehouse or godown 'which has just been erected at a cost of $1500, [and] is partly let to Chinamen at the extravagant rate of $250 per month for half of it'.

By the time the Small Knife Society's rebellion ended some 20,000 Chinese were living in the settlements, hoping for security for their lives and their possessions. The wealthy among them had been targeted by both the rebels and the imperial troops. An elderly Chinese friend of Thomas's, Yang Ta-foong, had been ruined by both sides:

the rebels made him pay £100,000 when they had him in the city, and the Mandarins came down on him for £70,000 more, when the city was captured for having supplied the rebels (though forced to it) with the former amount.[9]

The chaos and tragedy of war were not limited to China, and neither was the potential for profit. In 1861 the US Civil War began. The southern states had supplied the cotton for the mills of Britain and now the flow of cotton ceased. Thomas, with his intelligence and his keen eye for opportunity, saw his chance. Cotton was one of the major agricultural crops grown around Shanghai, but it was traded on the domestic market alone. The foreign traders had previously taken no interest in it. Now, according to a Mr Batchelor, once a colleague of Thomas's in Shanghai, the Civil War became for Thomas:

the greatest indirect source of his exceptional fortune, for he was the first to discern the effect it would have upon the supplies of cotton and by a stroke of genius he bought up all obtainable. It had not been exported before.[10]

As Stella Dong remarks in her book on the history of the city:

By the end of 1861, more than three million pounds sterling had accumulated in the hands of cotton's 'lucky buyers' and the fluffy white stuff had become Shanghai's number one export.[11]

Thomas now had the capital at his disposal to start developing the property portfolio that was to make him the largest private landowner in Shanghai.

The Taiping Rebellion was continuing. The threat that it posed was on a far grander scale than the Small Knife Society's had been and by 1862 the Chinese population in the British Settlement had risen to 50,000. In April 1861 Thomas had written that he considered Shanghai to be overwhelmed by people. The streets were practically impassable, so thick were the throngs of refugees. He estimated that the population would reach 500,000 by Christmas. In 1864 the combined figure given for the number of Chinese living in the foreign settlements in Shanghai was 150,000. The price of property rocketed. An acre of land in 1850 cost an average of £50, but by the early 1860s the price had increased to anywhere between £12,000 and £20,000, according to some sources. The kindness and honesty that Thomas had always shown to the Chinese in business meant that it was to him that many wealthy Chinese turned in these desperate times:

I have the honour of having great confidence placed in me by wealthy Chinese at this crisis: at least one hundred thousand pounds' worth of silk, treasure, trinkets, fur dresses, etc., have been deposited with me for safe keeping. I am daily begged the favour of being allowed to remain on our premises in case of any attack, and I have no doubt, on such attack occurring, I should have at least two hundred men and women around me. They are quite ready to pay for accommodation but I think it mean to ask.[12]

Wealthy Chinese are so constantly asking me to help them to manage their property, to act for them, become trustee and all manner of things... actually the other day the title-deeds of no fewer than twenty-six landed properties...were put into my hands... the value of them all must have been over fifty thousand pounds.[13]

The Chinese merchants' esteem for Thomas appears to have been unique. Their faith, affection and trust went far beyond providing material goods. Thomas mixed socially with the Chinese, and not just the menfolk. On at least one occasion, for example, he entertained:

several wealthy Chinese silkmen, their wives and children ... you are doubtless aware of the extreme ignorance and seclusion in which Chinese women are kept and the jealousy with which they are watched; without conceit I believe I may say there is not another foreigner in Shanghae [*sic*] whom the natives trust as they do me to see their families, and I esteem it the highest compliment when a wealthy man the other day allowed his wives to come and see my house and take tiffin attended only by their waiting women. I never heard of such a thing before in Shanghae or elsewhere.[14]

There is a photograph of Thomas taken at this time. He stands on the steps outside his house, looking the very picture of Victorian manhood. A hearty pair of mutton-chop whiskers and a thick moustache obscures the lower part of his face. He wears a suit and waistcoat, tweed perhaps, and a watch chain loops across his abdomen. He has a hat on, of course, which looks like a flattened bowler. His hands are clasped behind his back. It is a group portrait and Thomas stands to the far right of the ensemble. The other members of the group are all Chinese and of 15 adults all but four are women. The ladies are seated according to degree, all adorned in sumptuous apparel. The black and white tones inevitably dull the lustre of the ladies' ornate and rich silks, but not the sense of occasion. It was an afternoon when the company was, Thomas recorded, 'excessively merry and indeed laughed beyond all bounds. I suppose it was the novelty!' The photograph dates from 1864 and is an extraordinary visual testament to Thomas's standing among the Chinese in Shanghai.

Entertainments were provided in honour of Thomas as well. For his birthday in July 1861 the Chinese merchants threw a party that lasted from nine in the evening until four the next morning. Fifty or 60 Chinese guests attended, including 20 ladies, who were separated from the men by a calico sheet strung across the room. The banquet was a fusion of East and West, including delicacies as diverse as deer's tendons and that fine British dish, a plate of ginger nuts. Throughout the party a band accompanied a Chinese historical drama enacted by 44 performers. According to Thomas, 'The Chinamen say, since the English fleet came to Shanghai, no Englishman has received such a compliment.'[15]

Thomas's increasing respect for, and friendship with, the Chinese did nothing to lessen his sense of isolation from many elements of western behaviour in China. In a letter dated 26 April 1861 he relates:

> My Chinese friends here quite overwhelm me with kindness. I am sure I shall never be so well treated in any other part of the world I may go hereafter. How strangely these people are maligned and misrepresented in England!

He goes on to say that 'the policy pursued by England towards China during the past twenty-two years presents one of the darkest pages in our annals'.

Such was Thomas's standing among the Chinese that when, in November 1861, the Taiping rebels sought to communicate with the representatives of the European powers in Shanghai, they did so through him. Thomas was under no illusion as to the brutal nature of China's government and its deep-rooted corruption, but neither did he harbour prejudices in favour of the West. He noted the inhuman violence and cruelty dealt out by the British and French troops, the moral hypocrisy of the opium trade, and the absence of conscience in the dealings of most of the European traders. All that he witnessed in China called into question his nation's colonial and mercantile strategies. As western trade began to take hold in the long-isolated islands of Japan, Thomas wrote to his brother Daniel, on 3 February 1859, about a conversation he had had with Lord Elgin, the British representative during the negotiations with Japan:

> Lord Elgin told me in conversation that the forcing open of that country to our commerce cost him the greatest struggle that he had ever sustained; he found the Japanese so happy, contented and free from the vices which stain our civilisation, that it did seem a shame to disturb them. I can appreciate his feelings, and firmly believe that the Japanese will not derive the slightest benefit, at all events, for long to come, by contact with us, but probably a great deal of harm instead. A great deal of rubbish is talked in England about the blessings of civilisation etc.

Thomas refers to Japan, but this passage is surely a reflection of his experiences in China. The 'greatest struggle' lay in the conflict between conscience and purse. Thomas was in China to make himself an honest fortune. The opportunities in China that allowed for this were inextricably linked with the political machinations that he so deplored. However honourable, charitable and Christian Thomas's dealings were, his very presence in China implicated him by association with the cynical practices of his European colleagues.

Their cynicism reached its peak as the murderous Taiping rebels threatened Shanghai and the Settlements, laying waste to the surrounding areas: some of the European traders actually supplied them with muskets and ammunition. An elderly musket might fetch as much as $100. In 1862 it was discovered that one Shanghai company had sold the Taiping more than 3,000 assorted muskets, shotguns, pistols and rifles.[16] The rebels persecuted the local population and robbed them of everything they owned. Thomas viewed his fellow traders with disgust. On 29 October he records in a letter that:

> Foreigners continue to sell them [the Rebels] arms and gun-
> powder etc and realise enormous profits and the first houses in
> the place do not consider it beneath them to buy the silk (ridicu-
> lously cheap) that they have stolen from the unfortunate country
> people.

Everywhere the Chinese people were being cheated and betrayed by
westerners. A dispirited and overworked Thomas writes on 22
December 1861: 'inwardly I vow, over and over again, I will cut the
business altogether after 1865'.[17] A month later Thomas surveys the
human tragedy of the war:

> I must have seen twenty or thirty thousand of the peasantry who
> had been driven from their homes, and were lying about in the
> open country with their wives and children, and the small por-
> tion of worldly effects they had been able to carry away: the after-
> noon and succeeding night were bitterly cold, and though they
> sought to shelter themselves on the lee side of the mounds of
> earth [graves], I fear that several must have died. I saw nothing of
> the rebels, but heard a party of horsemen approached within a
> mile of our Settlement, and murdered some poor old women, the
> bodies being frightfully mutilated.[18]

The dangers to life and limb were not confined to those presented
by the Taiping rebels. Shanghai, as Thomas had observed on his
arrival in 1853, was still little more than a swamp. Ague (malaria)
was, along with typhoid, the most common malady. The house that
Thomas lived in for the first years of his tenure was named Mosquito
Lodge. Hoping to be met by William Crampton on the quayside, the

young entrepreneurs had been informed that he was incapacitated by fever and could not leave his bed. Within a year (as mentioned above) Charles Pullan, another partner, was so stricken with dysentery that he was unable to work and was eventually invalided back to Britain. The public sewerage system for Shanghai was ancient, unhealthy and troublesome. Traditionally all waste was either collected by night-soilers for manure or simply drained into the fine network of rivers, canals, dykes and creeks that spread across the land. The Shanghai swamp, like all swamps, did not drain with any great alacrity and the system had, of course, been developed for a city of a much smaller population than the 400,000 who were living there by the 1840s. The ditches and marshy creeks around the city were becoming blocked. In 1851 a Chinese magistrate had taken the matter in hand and dredged these 'drains', only to dump the cleared filth by the city walls. The rapid growth of the foreign settlements and the floods of refugees that fled the Taiping rebels exacerbated an already difficult situation. The archaic Chinese system was put under even greater strain by the massive building programme undertaken by the Europeans. In the pursuit of property and profit, drains and ditches were regularly filled in as the settlements expanded. Dysentery and chronic diarrhoea became commonplace.[19]

The health of Thomas and his associates is a regular topic in his correspondence, and for good reason:

Many people have been ill and several have died, a day or two ago there were three ladies all lying dead at one time, and Mrs Winch, a lady universally liked here, is now in a most precarious state and I fear cannot recover. If she dies it will be three out of one house in the course of as many months.[20]

Thomas's evidently weakened state on his return home in 1858 and the dogged recurrence of ill health seem to have been an accepted part of Shanghai life:

My health remains about as before neither better nor worse, except the bleeding to which I was subject at home has begun afresh but I do not know that there is much to be alarmed at in that.[21]

There was the constant possibility of falling prey to an illness that would prove fatal, or necessitate repatriation and a lifetime of debilitation. The steady accumulation of displaced Chinese in Shanghai and the settlements, combined with the rudimentary state of public healthcare, brought about the inevitable. Between 1862 and 1863 Shanghai suffered a cholera epidemic. At its height, in July 1863, an estimated one to two thousand Chinese were dying from the disease each day in the Shanghai region. For the foreigners the number of fatalities was considerably lower, but proportionate to the size of the foreign population the figure was substantial nonetheless. Cholera had no respect for extraterritoriality. On 18 February 1863 Thomas reported to Daniel:

You would scarcely credit the fact that sixteen hundred Europeans were buried here over the past year; the cemeteries are rapidly filling up and new ones to be made.

Sickness in many forms abounded in Shanghai and it was another hardship that constantly confronted Thomas:

I wrote Papa on the 2nd and 3rd inst. about poor young Satow: I then had very good hopes of his recovery, but soon after a low typhoid fever seized him; this, coming when he was frightfully low from the effects of cholera, he was unable to bear up against it. We nursed him night and day incessantly, feeding him with nourishing food and stimulants every twenty minutes, but our care was unavailing and he died on the evening of the 13th inst. I write by the present opportunity both to his father and mother, to whom I fear it will be a great blow.[22]

One of our coolies was seized with cholera the other evening; symptoms: cramps in the legs, vomiting, extremeties cold and no pulse. As the doctors do not seem to be of much use, I thought I would try and bring him round myself, and rubbed his stomach and chest with slices of green ginger, then applied very strong mustard poultices to his stomach and the calves of his legs; in an hour and a half the pulse returned: in three hours more circulation recommenced actively in the extremeties; and by the following morning he seemed out of danger and is now convalescent. The only medicine I gave him was eighty drops of chlorodyne in five hours.[23]

Thomas's care for the sick did not stop at nursing those around him. The London Mission Hospital in Shanghai had been founded by missionaries in 1844 for the treatment of Chinese patients. Known from its beginnings as the Chinese Hospital, it was kept solvent by charitable subscription. Thomas was a great financial supporter of this institution and it exerted, perhaps, the single most positive influence on Anglo-Chinese relations ever contrived by the British. Thanks to the incredible industry of the likes of Dr Edward Henderson and Keith and Chin Foo, 100,000 patients were treated between 1860 and 1864, and during those years 20,000 immunizations were carried out in the vaccination clinic. By the early 1870s supplies of equipment, drugs and cash were becoming scarce. Thomas Hanbury was then the Chairman of the Hospital Committee. At this time of need he provided all the drugs and equipment necessary, and regularly continued to do so from then on. In times of further financial difficulties, such as in 1874, when Thomas was no longer resident in China, he could still be relied on to provide a vital contribution to the new Chinese Hospital. Diseases and afflictions of the eyes were desperately common among the Chinese of that period. Thomas was instrumental in setting up a clinic, the Agnes Gutslaff Ophthalmic Hospital, to specialize in the treatment of ophthalmic disorders.

Thomas's accounting and business skills made him a most useful committee member. His unprejudiced straight talking and the bluntness of his style did not always make him popular with the established members of the community, or its press:

> Our annual meeting of the land renters took place the other day, when the municipal council presented the budget for the coming year, a monstrous one it seemed to me, since it proposed to increase the expenditure and consequent taxation from £60,000 per annum to £100,000 for our Settlement alone... I offered a resolution opposing the budget and carried it, so the 'ministry' was thrown out. The increased taxation it was proposed the Chinese alone should bear, which I considered very unjust. I send you 'Friend of China' to show you the style of abuse indulged in by this valuable periodical against myself.[24]

As he was now the largest individual property-owner in Shanghai, Thomas's opinions commanded attention. He was elected Treasurer to the Council and helped to see the Settlement through the harsh economic downturn that beset Shanghai in 1864–5. Without his stand against the Council's reckless budget, the Settlement might have faced bankruptcy. The assembled company had accepted all of Thomas's financial proposals. Having been elected to the Council, Thomas then had to implement a budget of his own. His new responsibilities were time-consuming and often frustrating:

These municipal matters take up much of my time and as Shanghai is not amenable to any code of laws and the payment of taxes is quite voluntary, you may imagine the job of collecting some £70,000 per annum is no sinecure.[25]

Thomas's vision of the political structure of the Shanghai Municipal Council did not meet with such approval. A piece of foxed card left with letters written to his brother Daniel in 1864 is dated 16 April that year. On it, written in Thomas's clear handwriting, can be read:

Resolution moved by T. Hanbury at meeting of land renters – 'That with the object of having the native Residents and tax payers represented at the Council Board and thus gaining more correct information regarding Chinese affairs generally, it is desirable at this time to elect two Chinamen of known wealth and independent position to the Council for the ensuing year.'[26]

The resolution was not carried.

The most eloquent testament to Thomas's political efforts on behalf of the Chinese appears in one of the many farewell gifts presented to him by grateful Chinese friends and traders when he left Shanghai in April 1866. He was not sure if he would ever return, although he placated his Chinese friends' fears by saying that he might be back within three years. He left Shanghai emotionally and physically exhausted, and extremely rich. Before he departed he was so overwhelmed by gifts from his Chinese friends and acquaintances that he was forced to plead with them to bring a halt to the train of presents. The most moving gifts were two dedicatory epistles extolling the virtues of Thomas, the affections of his friends and the deep sadness of his leaving. One was from a group of 28 assorted merchants, the second, quoted here in translation, from the Chinese silk merchants of Shanghai. I consider it to be not only evidence for Thomas's commitment to defending the rights of the Chinese, but also a succinct and true description of the noble and superior qualities that he possessed:

> Mr Thomas Hanbury, an English merchant, has resided in China for over ten years, he is acquainted with the customs, manners and character of the Chinese; in his dealings with men he is faithful, worthy of respect, and a pattern of what is good. The abolition of the tax on market men and native cargo boats, the equitable management of the municipal house tax, and abolition of the night pass system are instances of his praiseworthy deeds.
>
> Whatever he has ability to do he always does with earnestness. He is a friend to those in trouble, and a peacemaker to those who quarrel, and never was he known to use his power for the oppression of any person.
>
> His mode of living is economical and plain; his wisdom and judgement are of a high order; these are the secrets of his commercial success.[27]

Thomas wrote a final letter to his brother Daniel on the day he left Shanghai, 22 April 1866: 'Today, my last day in Shanghai, began with rain, but it has now cleared up and the sun is shining brightly; this is emblematical of my career in China.'[28]

The misery and hardship of the early years of Shanghai had gone, leaving Thomas wealthy and respected by both Chinese and European citizens of Shanghai. Thomas had made his fortune without it costing him his body or his soul: other western traders in Shanghai tended to lose at least one of these. The moral contradictions that had been apparent to Thomas, as he strove to follow a righteous path in the pursuit of riches, were not to disappear. As this book will make apparent, unlike the clouds and rain of 22 April some of the darker elements of Shanghai were to linger and cast the occasional shadow later in Thomas's life. The acquisition of a fortune is not a pursuit for the faint-hearted and unambitious, and is, perhaps, never free of moral ambiguity. Thomas, however, had demonstrated an outstanding sense of charity and compassion throughout his time in Shanghai, distinguishing himself markedly from his peers. Thomas's Christian faith, his adherence to his Quaker beliefs about the proper treatment of his fellow human beings, sets him apart from the other traders. A steeliness runs through both his industry and his humanity, a core of determined self-belief. Thomas rarely wavered.

A final anecdote is taken from a letter to his brother Daniel dated 10 January 1860. It concerns neither his business affairs nor his charitable works. The passage describes Thomas at play and is not without some emblematic qualities of its own. Even in the proud and absurd ritual of the Englishman abroad, Thomas's relentless determination is overwhelming. He carries on when his compatriots have given up and, having enlisted the support of the local Chinese, gleefully wins the day:

The other day I went out into the country with the beagles, a

pack of dogs kept by a gentleman here; we hunted all the afternoon unsuccessfully, but at last we came to three large coffins
standing together, built up with brickwork partly in a decayed
state: the dogs made a great noise and we felt there must be some
animal under the coffins. We numbered about twelve gentlemen
and fifteen dogs; there were about one hundred villagers near by
watching our proceedings; all the rest were afraid to rout out the
animal for fear of rousing the anger of the peasantry by disturbing the tombs, and nobody could speak to them but myself; after
trying in vain for five minutes or so, they all went away; I therefore was determined to get the animal out, so called to the peasants to bring spades to help me; they came willingly and we dug
away at the brick rubbish, and on looking underneath I saw the
tail of what I took to be a wild cat. I poked at it and out it ran
on the other side across a field and over a creek, with myself and
villagers in full pursuit; there was a Chinese dog nearby who
seized it and killed it at once; it proved to be a civet and measured, I should say, two feet from tip of nose to end of tail. The
rest of the party were somewhat chagrined to find that I had got
it alone with one Chinese dog, while they with their fifteen
beagles were unsuccessful![29]

# Chapter Five
# Riviera Robinson Crusoe

'I am determined that I will not slave anymore after I am 35 or
40 years of age; if I am then not rich enough to be independent
in a civilised country I will go to the Fee-jees or some out of the
way place and there live in a primitive Robinson Crusoe style.'

Thus wrote Thomas Hanbury to his mother on 31 July 1861. Five
years later he had returned home from China a man of substance,
aged 34. For the time being, at least, he had retired from his active
partnership in Bower, Hanbury & Co. Thomas was worn out. He
had accumulated a large fortune in a very short time, but the sheer
industry involved had proved exhausting. He had survived the
unhealthy swamps of Shanghai, but his health was weak. Thomas was
an asthmatic and bronchial problems were to dog him throughout his
life. Even in February 1868 Thomas replied to an inquiry from a colleague as to his possible return to Shanghai:

Lately I have been strongly advised against such a step by all my
near relations who almost without exception, think my health is
not sufficiently strong and re-established to warrant my taking

such labour and responsibility...

Thomas had been a witness to death and human tragedy on a scale beyond the comprehension of his peers at home. He wrote on his last day in Shanghai that he felt 'rather melancholy and like a fish out of water in going away from Shanghai'.[1] It was a feeling that was not to diminish once he was home in England. He was, of course, overjoyed to see his family and friends once more, and the summer and autumn of 1866 saw an unending stream of family gatherings and parties. All of Thomas's hardship and toil in Shanghai had brought him to this desired point: wealthy retirement at a young age. The idyll was not yet realized, however. For all the property that Thomas owned in Shanghai, he lacked a house of his own in Britain. More importantly, a truth that Thomas acknowledged to his friends was that, as a young single man in possession of a good fortune, he was most certainly in want of a wife. After years of bachelorhood in Shanghai, Thomas yearned for a suitable Mrs Hanbury. Thomas wrote with typical honesty and humour to his friend Brenier on Boxing Day 1866:

I came home with quite the idea and wish of finding someone of congenial mind and of similar tastes and ideas who I might make the future Mrs H. but in this I regret to say I have completely failed. It is a great disappointment to me, but I suppose it is my own fault in being too critical and fastidious. Of course I have met dozens, perhaps hundreds, of beautiful and amiable young ladies, and being considered by the majority of Papas and Mamas quite elligible it would be strange if I experienced any difficulty in getting married. What I complain of is that young ladies in England at present have too much degenerated into very elegant pegs on which are hung the most splendid dresses that trail along the ground, and whose heads are decorated with enormous chignons, surmounted by fabulously small bonnets, they play on the piano and sing to perfection, but when one looks for the more stirring qualities of the heart they are either wanting or concealed with such care that it is impossible to tell whether they exist or not. I really do not believe that there is one young lady out of ten, who before she is engaged cares anything for the young man she accepts. What then happens? If fortunate he succeeds in gaining her affection afterwards, but if not there is misery and unhappiness for both. This is what I decline to run the risk of.

Thomas loathed the English winter, with its 'choking fog and cheerless sky', and was clearly dispirited by the apparent lack of marital prospects. The pattern of life and excitement that Shanghai had provided had now slipped away. Naturally, he remained in contact with his ex-partner and the agents who dealt with his huge property portfolio in China, but the retirement dream had lost its lustre. Hardly anyone in England seemed the least bit interested in China, yet China was always on Thomas's mind. The sense of isolation returned. Thomas was listless, bored and unhappy, and his asthmatic tendencies were aggravated by the damp London air. His brother Daniel suggested a holiday, not to 'the Fee-jees' but to the Continent, specifically the stretch of coast between Nice in France and San Remo in Italy.

The French coastline had first caught the eye of travelling Britons in the 18th century. Tobias Smollett is often credited with first bringing Nice and Menton to the attention of sickly Britons fleeing the unpleasantness of northern winters. In 1763 Smollett had himself gone there for reasons of health and had written a caustically entertaining account of his sojourn. His satirical and choleric eye was brought to bear on the natives and their customs, but the advantages of a Mediterranean sun for those used to North Sea fogs were unassailable. The numbers of wintering Britons steadily increased. The arrival of Lord Brougham in Cannes in 1834 established the Côte d'Azur as a popular winter resort for the wealthy British.

By the 1850s the British were moving east. Away from Nice, past the great rock of Monaco, past Cap St Martin, the British found Menton. Menton lies in a particularly sheltered cove, tucked in between the shore and the mountains that rise steeply behind. Viewed today from the Ponte San Luigi, which takes the high road into Italy, the old town of Menton still looks utterly charming. The church tower standing clear above the tiled roofs holds the eye and unifies the cluster of softly coloured stone buildings, patterned by shutters, as they shuffle down to the sea. The town is best seen in the light of early morning or late afternoon. The low sun makes the stone glow and lessens the impact of the cluttered marina, lying in the foreground like a watery caravan park. The experience is undoubtedly enhanced by an aperitif; a small café has been thoughtfully provided. I am reliably informed that the average time a privately owned French boat spends at sea each year is 40 minutes.

One hundred and fifty years ago the small harbour of Menton was busy with boats trading, ferrying, fishing and smuggling. A terminally ill Dr J.H. Bennet arrived in Menton in 1859, hoping to find a quiet and comfortable spot to end his days. Far from easing himself into Death's embrace in a bath chair on the esplanade at Menton, Dr Bennet found the climate so conducive to good health that he quite recovered. He went on to extol the virtues of Menton's benevolent air to his patients in London and to the literate members of the English-speaking world through his book *Winter on the Shores of the Mediterranean* (1875), first published as *Mentone and the Riviera as a Winter Climate* in 1861. It proved a very popular book and ran to several editions. Thomas was to require Dr Bennet's services himself in 1867, due to 'a bad attack of spasmodic asthma'. It was after a thorough examination by Bennet, on 2 April, that Thomas first visited the renowned garden that the doctor had made near the frontier. Bennet became a friend and horticultural ally to Thomas. During the 1860s Bennet had contributed occasional articles to *The Gardener's Chronicle* about his Riviera garden. These were articles that Dr Spruce recommended to Daniel as most useful for the task of making the garden at La Mortola. From Thomas's diary it is possible to see that, as time passed, it was Bennet who increasingly consulted his sometime patient. On 27 April 1878, in a typically economical note, Thomas records: 'Dr Bennet called and related his matrimonial troubles.[2]

The success of Dr Bennet's book had a huge impact on Menton over the next 40 years, as the town transformed itself into a thriving resort, particularly favoured by the British. The touristic profile of Menton was raised to heights previously undreamt of by Queen Victoria's residency there during her holiday in 1882. Such was the municipal gratitude to Dr Bennet that on 13 December 1894 a memorial bust of him was erected in Menton.

By the time that Thomas arrived, in the spring of 1867, Menton had gently established itself as an English resort. Thomas left London on 9 March and by the end of the month was in Menton, resident at the Hotel de la Grande Bretagne, its name evidence enough of an English invasion. Thomas was struck by the beauty of his surroundings. His mood began to lift and, after only two days, he began to view local property with an eye to a purchase. Menton sits on the border between France and Italy. After a few forays to Roquebrune, Monaco and St Agnes, Thomas turned to Italy and crossed the border to visit Ventimiglia and Bordighera. Travelling by carriage, Thomas would have passed through the little village of La Mortola Inferiore and more than likely caught a glimpse of the sturdy back of the Palazzo Orengo, or the Villa Grandis as it was then known. It is not known whether Thomas formed any opinion of the property then, but on 25 March the house and its land were to make so powerful an impression on him that, little more than a month later, he became the new proprietor at La Mortola.

For the English visitors to Menton, and especially those who patronized the Hotel de la Grande Bretagne, the ramshackle Villa Grandis had been a favourite picnic spot for some years. Situated a mile or two along the coast from Menton, the villa sat above a small headland, and surveyed a striking view of the coast and sea. Parties would take a boat to the small beach on the eastern side of the property. Those inclined to bathe could do so and then ascend to the dishevelled, ancient Palazzo for an *al-fresco* lunch. The residents of the Hotel de la Grande Bretagne often favoured this excursion: the landlord's aunt, Signora Grandis, was the owner of the villa and was in search of a buyer. Thomas was curious to view some Italian villas that were on the market and, to that end, on 25 March he and three other British visitors were taken by boat from Menton.

The terracotta palazzo, viewed from the sea, emerges from a great green scree of foliage that flows down the hillside, while above and to the right stands La Mortola Inferiore. The little cape is thickly planted and verdant, free of the buildings that stud the hillsides running across to the cape at Bordighera. Treading water in the

Mediterranean, with one's eyes only an inch or two above sea level, accentuates the dramatic 300-foot rise of the garden from the shore to the Corso Monte Carlo and serves as a reminder of just how isolated La Mortola must have been in 1867. Nearly 150 years after Thomas first set foot on the headland, it is hard to appreciate the great changes that have occurred. Fortunately, Daniel Hanbury preserved the scene in a watercolour painted in July 1867. The garden then appeared as a series of regular but ragged terraces of olive trees stretching back up the hillside, while towards the lower parts, below the house, there were unkempt plots of vegetables with shambolic orchards of lemons, assorted fruit trees and vines. Beneath the citrus and olive trees, in whites and greys, there was a liberal sprinkling of sheep and goats, browsing slowly, methodically and ruthlessly on all available greenery. A thick wall enclosed the property from the sea. An irregular avenue of cypress led down to the old Roman road that cuts through the property a little way up from the sea.

The Palazzo Orengo sat on the eastern edge of the land, on a massive rampart faced with stone. The palazzo was not large – it has been called a *palazzini* – and it has also been described as a typical Ligurian cube. Its style was plain and robust, its two floors surmounted by a stunted tower. The house commands a superlative site, one that proclaims its past as a fortification against Saracen pirates. In Daniel's painting one can make out the rounded head of the single date palm that stood just to the west of the house and was remarked on by Thomas. The palm was, perhaps, another memento of the Saracen influence on the Ligurian coast. The condition of the roof and various ceilings varied between partial and total disrepair. The palazzo was in a state of advanced decrepitude and a home to livestock rather than local nobility. Much of the hillside was steep, rocky and ill-suited to cultivation, other than that of olives. Whatever its imagined state, however, it is certain that Thomas conceived an uncharacteristic passion for La Mortola with characteristic decisiveness.

The following excerpts from Thomas's letters provide an excellent description of the property as he saw it. They illustrate the renewal of his sense of risk and adventure, and the development of a profound personal response to his investment:

I have taken a great liking to this part of Europe which is called the Riviera, it enjoys the most delicious climate winter and summer, the olive, lemon, orange, loquat, cactus, aloe etc etc flourish in the open air, the scenery is most charming and the people a simple industrious, well behaved race. Notwithstanding all these advantages you will be perhaps hardly prepared to learn that I have purchased an estate and that the Palazzo Orengo, two miles this side of Menton became mine yesterday. As regards scenery I consider it the pick of all the places I have seen along this coast and as near perfection as possible. Of course there are some disadvantages, the situation is retired. I have cape Mortola to myself and there are no English within two miles. I am half a mile in Italy, just across the new boundary established after the peace of Villafranca. I have a palace it is true but it bears a striking resemblance to a barn with rooms at present. There are about 10 acres of land and my garden produces lemons, oranges, pomegranites, Figs, Cherries, Grapes, Pears, Olives, Peaches, Strawberries etc in abundance and a magnificent Palm tree rears its head at the side of the house. Looking out of the windows on a clear day one sees across the Mediterranean the snow capped peaks of Corsica, to the east along the Italian coast are the ancient and picturesque towns of Ventimiglia & Bordighera within easy distance.

On the west the town of Mentone in a charming bay, Monaco the smallest principality in the world, the bay of Nice and the Estrelles mountains in the distance. On the North behind the house, the olive woods cover the hills, but the charming little tower to the village church of Mortola appears to great advantage among the trees. I look on the place as a retreat to be used only occasionally by myself or friends when wishing to escape the severity of an English winter.[3]

You will perceive from the dating of this letter that I am actually in 'my palace'. I did not hesitate to come here alone although I cannot speak Italian and my French is extremely limited. I wanted to see and understand the people and the means of subsistence consequently eschewing all imported servants. I engaged a shepherdess who I found tending her sheep and goats in a field at the bottom of my garden, she cooks for me and her brother who is a fisherman supplies me with what he catches just in sight of my house. Thus I am having a sort of picnic, a contented mind, brilliant weather, and charming scenery making amends for homeliness of fare. My first dinner consisted of Bread, Eggs, Wine of the Country and Goat's Milk, but today there is a decided improvement fish, mutton, Butter, cheese and loquats (Chinese Pe bo) now rife in my Garden. The repairs will cost me a large sum but the place will be very nice when they are finished and the garden somewhat put in order.[4]

The dourness and low spirits that Thomas expressed in London had vanished, and been replaced by excitement and joy in this romantic idyll. In a letter to his business partner Frederick Bower, Thomas admits: 'I bought the place because I took a violent fancy to it'. Thomas had fallen in love but, of course, he was unwilling to describe a property purely in terms of aesthetics and desire. The sentence continues:

> and [I] believe it will pay as an investment if I never use it, but I think that many of my friends will like occasionally to come there to escape the severity of an English winter and as the railway will soon be completed the place will shortly be within 48 hours of London.[5]

Thomas could see how the popularity of the Ligurian coast was set to grow rapidly. Italy had long been established as the ultimate destination for any Briton indulging in that cultural rite of passage, the Grand Tour. However, it was the artistic and historical lodestones, such as Rome and Florence that had been the main draw. In the 1860s Italy had become Britain's favourite foreign country in the world for another reason entirely: while imperial China was beginning to implode, Italy spent the 19th century being reborn.

After the continental turmoil of the Napoleonic era, and the political and diplomatic settlement that ensued, Italy had continued its existence as a disparate group of states and principalities dominated by the Austrians. By 1866, however, Italy had seen the last of a series of three wars of independence and unification that had captured the sympathies of the English public in an unprecedented manner. In the eyes of many the plucky Italian underdog not only brought eventual defeat to the arrogant and oppressive Austrians, but also embodied the pure aspirations of 19th-century nationalism, the expression of which impressed and delighted no people more than the British. The spiritual and physical emblem, the human incarnation, of all this nobility, patriotism and valour was Giuseppe Garibaldi. In 1860 even Thomas's politically reticent brother Daniel had been inspired to write:

> The news from Sicily attracts much attention and Garibaldi and his followers have the sympathy of most Englishmen and the pecuniary assistance of a few. The insurrection has taken such a hold that the island whether it becomes a part of Sardinia or not, can scarcely return to Neapolitan rule, and in fact the government is so execrable that any change the Sicilians get will be for their benefit rather than otherwise.[6]

It is in the public adoration of Garibaldi that the best indication of the passionate British support for the *Risorgimento* can be witnessed. In 1854 the working men of Newcastle upon Tyne subscribed to present Garibaldi with a gift, while in 1861 17,000 inhabitants of Brighton contributed a penny each for the same end. In 1864 Garibaldi visited Britain and was fêted in an unprecedented frenzy. Even the huge significance of his inspecting the British Fleet at the Isle of Wight pales in comparison to the ecstatic scenes in London, where 600,000 people packed the streets to bid him welcome. The *Daily Telegraph* was moved to describe it as 'the most memorable ovation that has ever been given at any period of the world's history'.[7] Garibaldi could be said to have been the Nelson Mandela of Victorian Britain and Italy rode high in the consciousness of the British people.

The stretch of coast on which Thomas was now resident was increasing in popularity with the British, but not only for its proximity to Menton. A few miles east along the bay was the village of Bordighera. It had been of little interest to English visitors until the publication of the novel *Dr Antonio*, in 1855. Written by Giovanni Ruffini, known as the 'Patriot of Taggia', *Dr Antonio* was a winning mixture of romance and patriotic duty that appealed enormously to British Risorgophiles. An aristocratic English Rose, travelling in Italy with her crusty father, is forced after a coaching accident to accept treatment by the handsome and noble Dr Antonio in the tiny village of Bordighera. Here she must rest and recuperate for long enough to fall in love with the dashing doctor, and, of course, with the notion of a free and united Italy. Even the Tory baronet finds his reactionary politics softening under the Mediterranean sun, and in the face of the irreproachable goodness and humanity of the liberal doctor. The book contains many descriptions of Bordighera's natural endowments of benign climate and natives. Within two or three years of its publication the previously insignificant village and palm plantation could boast a Hotel d'Angleterre. It was soon to become the Italian Menton.

There were those who insisted, with some vigour, that the French town of Menton was in fact the Italian town of Mentone. The coastline from Ventimiglia to Nice had been subjected to frequent changes of nationality and allegiance over the centuries, and then the tremendous upheavals of the Risorgimento had their effects in turn on the political geography of the Riviera. Thomas writes of La Mortola being only half a mile inside Italy following the Treaty of Villafranca. As a result of French assistance against the Austrians in 1859, this treaty ceded land from Nizza to Mentone to France, thereby transforming them into Nice and Menton. Thus despite Garibaldi, the ultimate Italian patriot, having been born in Nizza; his birthplace was now officially Nice.

National boundaries were only one part of the problem. The celebrated analysis of the Risorgimento by one of its leading figures, Mazzini – 'We have made Italy but we have yet to make Italians' –

neatly expresses how Italy's transition to nationhood had bypassed some of its natives. Nothing quite illustrates the complexity of the emergent Italy's difficulties, as does the issue of language. If a country's people are bound together by anything, if a nation can be said to have a sense of common identity, then a shared language must be one of the most basic of adhesives. At the time that Thomas was settling into La Mortola most Italians did not actually speak Italian: indeed, only 2.5 per cent of the 26.8 million members of the new Italy knew what became standard Italian and, if the inhabitants of Tuscany and Rome are removed from the statistics, the figure drops to a quite staggering 0.6 per cent. The vast majority spoke only regional dialects. Even King Victor Emmanuel II conducted cabinet meetings in Piedmontese.[8]

Italian as a language existed on paper, to be read but rarely spoken. Unfortunately, most Italians were illiterate. In 1871 68.8 per cent of the population were unable to read:

> As long as 'Italian' remained only a written language, to be illiterate was to be ignorant of Italian. Conversely, since school readers and textbooks were written in Italian, and since the medium of instruction in schools was supposed to be Italian, to be ignorant of Italian was to be, and to remain, ignorant.[9]

The 'making of Italians' was to be engineered in schools, but the public school system was erratic to say the least. The town councils or *communi* were made responsible for providing a basic primary education in 1859. Like everything else, however, the implementation of this policy was utterly dependent on the locality and the members of each commune.

Thomas had demonstrated in Shanghai that his perspective on life was broad. He always appreciated that there existed beyond the boundaries of the Settlement not merely a selection of profit-making opportunities, but a great and ancient empire, a people and their culture. On his arrival in Italy his attitude was just the same. As quoted above, he wanted to 'see and understand the people and the means of subsistence'. It did not take long for him to understand the poverty in which these people lived. By 9 May 1867 he had set up a girls' school in La Mortola. It was the first of many such acts. Thomas strongly believed that education was the key to economic and social improvement, and his charitable instincts were focused time and time again on this issue. The interests of the new Italian state and the beliefs of Thomas Hanbury shared a common purpose in the making of Italians.

At this stage Thomas still writes of La Mortola as an investment, a sometime holiday home for him and his friends, but the words seem to ring hollow. With hindsight it is hard to believe that the Palazzo Orengo was ever just an investment to Thomas. Perhaps he felt it necessary to include the 'investment' tag to remind his colleagues that, although he had fallen in love with a ruined Italian palazzo by the sea and was currently living a rural idyll there, being served cheese and wine by a local shepherdess, they should not be perplexed. He was still Thomas Hanbury, property magnate. Thomas thought of La Mortola as his home until his death in 1907. The founding of the girls' school, not six weeks after his first setting foot on Cap Mortola, was a statement of intent as well as charity. It represented a substantial commitment to the community of La Mortola.

Thomas returned to London on 13 May 1867, leaving Sebastiano Lorenzi in charge of the four men and six women whom Thomas had employed to carry out the reclamation and development of the garden. He left detailed written instructions for Lorenzi and engaged a firm of solicitors in Menton, Bourrit & Simmler, to manage his affairs and watch over the building renovations to the Palazzo. Thomas went back to Italy with his elder brother Daniel in early July. Thomas was aware that his colleagues in the China trade were keen to involve him again. His old partner Frederick Bower looked to have him back in Shanghai within a year, to allow Bower himself to retire, but La Mortola was proving a most welcome diversion from Shanghai business. Thomas now had his home, but it lacked a most vital component: a wife and family. However he had been revitalized by La Mortola. The melancholia had been replaced by his customary vim and determination. By September Thomas was engaged to Miss Katherine Aldam Pease.

Thomas had met Katherine almost immediately after his return to London. Eleven years younger than Thomas, but, like him, a member of a well-connected and celebrated Quaker family, Katherine was well-educated, and lacked the worldly vanities and shallowness that Thomas had railed against the previous December. In a letter to the very correspondent, Brenier, who had received the earlier complaint, Thomas wrote on Christmas Eve 1867:

> I also take the opportunity of asking you to accept a photograph of Miss Pease, the young lady to whom I expect to be married to next February or March. I have chosen goodness rather than beauty you see; in person Miss Pease is two or three inches shorter than I am, graceful in carriage, very fair, clean, light complexion, with very blue eyes, she has been most carefully brought up by her Father (her mother having died when she was an infant) a gentleman of independent fortune living near Bristol.
>
> She is totally above all the frivolities of most young ladies of the

present day, is a fair French, German, Latin & Greek scholar, is well read but has seen very little of the world and society generally. I think her temper and disposition as near perfection as possible. But then I suppose people would say I am prejudiced.

My marriage will not be an ambitious one for my intended has really scarcely any of what are called <u>accomplishments</u> and so is not well fitted to shine in society.

Any notion that Thomas had been seized by another 'violent fancy' is hard to justify from this passage. Thomas was making a very sound emotional investment, choosing a companion who was kind, intelligent and 'as near perfection as possible'. Katherine's lack of worldliness, perhaps her lack of accomplishments, made her less likely to be affected by the absence of established society at La Mortola. Katherine was certainly no drawing-room ornament. After their marriage, in March 1868, the couple left for La Mortola, to return to England for the summer. In August 1869 the Orient and business claimed Thomas once more, and the couple set off together for Shanghai. Katherine was undaunted by the prospect of a two-year spell in China and Thomas observed: 'Katherine bore the travelling quite as well as I did and proved a better sailor'.[10] Once in Shanghai, Katherine eschewed the services of a personal maid and took herself off on a 10-day trip around the countryside, unaccompanied by Thomas. It was while they were in Shanghai that Katharine gave birth to their first child, Cecil, on 10 March 1871. Miss Pease had proved a worthwhile and productive investment.

The bachelor who had left England for the Riviera in March 1867, feeling morose and sickly, returned again to Italy, in March 1868, as the owner of a palazzo and the proud husband of Katherine. It had proved a busy year and one might expect that Thomas, having achieved so much, would indulge in a restful retirement. Had that not been the plan, even if it might have meant moving to 'the Fee-jees'? Yet over the next 40 years not only did Thomas Hanbury improve the lives, present and future, of the local and extended Ligurian community; not only did he give money and support to numerous charitable concerns around the world; but he created the most celebrated garden and plant collection in southern Europe. Where most would have been prepared to construct an appropriately conservative landscape to complement the palazzo, Thomas was responsible for a garden that was to be fêted and patronized by sight-seers, horticulturalists, nobles, botanists and members of the royal families of Europe. It would have more than 5,000 visitors a year by the early 1900s. Thomas Hanbury created a beautiful private garden that was not only enjoyed by the public, but was revered by botanists. This is rare indeed.

# Chapter Six
## Inspiration

Without the life and influence of Daniel Hanbury, it is hard to imagine the garden at La Mortola. In fact one could hypothesize that Thomas would never have gone to the Riviera at all had it not been for Daniel. Suppositions such as these are unnecessary, however, for the plain fact is that Daniel was so vital both to the garden and to Thomas that any discussion of either would be empty without a close examination of Daniel's life.

Clapham Common appears an unlikely site of inspiration for the garden at La Mortola, but it was there that both Daniel and Thomas learned and developed an early appreciation of botany. The Common was a different entity then, lying beyond the London streets, the last vague suburb before the countryside proper began. Surrounded by farmland, the Common was wilder than it is now, with trees arranged in copses rather than lines. Thomas was a keen shot and spent many hours roaming the Common with a gun, shooting rabbits. The local commons never lost their appeal to Daniel. Even after 30 or 40 years of living in Clapham, Daniel would still botanize on his walks, taking meticulous notes in his clear and precise handwriting.

Horticulture was a favoured pastime of the Hanburys. The family was proud of its garden and Daniel was to maintain a garden at his parents' house for all his life, even annexing a willing neighbour's garden to increase the available space. Daniel also had two glasshouses packed with rare plants, of sufficient value to be gladly accepted by Kew on his death. The interest in plants was, however, inextricable from the family business. Plants were the backbone of most drugs, and botany is a skill that can be taught and demonstrated anywhere there is a plant, dead or alive. The Hanburys were surrounded by fields, and both Clapham and Wandsworth Commons were nearby. The close-knit kinship of blood, faith and business shared by the small community of Quaker pharmacists – the Hanburys, the Allens and the Christys – meant that family and friends who had a knowledge of, and interest in, botany were never far from Daniel and his younger brother. The family's friends included Henry Deane, Quaker and co-founder of the Pharmaceutical Society, who had owned a business in Clapham since 1837. He was a tremendous botanist and doubtless encouraged the boys' interest. Deane was responsible for the introduction to botany of one of the boys' cousins, Frederick Janson Hanbury, who was to go on to publish a number of botanical works.[1] Another cousin, Francis Alfred Hanbury, though a qualified barrister, decided that botany was a preferable career.

Daniel Bell and Rachel Hanbury had had six children: Daniel, Sampson, Thomas, Anna, Capel and Barclay. Daniel, the eldest, was born in September 1825 and, like Thomas, was educated at the Quaker school at Croydon. One obituary of Daniel remarks that the school was not renowned for its academic brilliance, but, whatever its failings, Daniel left Croydon at the age of 16 with his keen, analytical mind unblunted and with a talent for watercolour painting. His responsibilities as eldest son were clear, and in 1841 he started his career as a pharmacist in the family firm of Allen & Hanbury. At the time Daniel began working, the pharmacy trade was experiencing a period of significant change: and it was a transition led by the Hanbury family. The year that Daniel joined Allen & Hanbury's Pharmacy his father, along with Cornelius Hanbury and William Allen, founded the Pharmaceutical Society. Until 1841 the trade had been an ill-defined group of specialists and shopkeepers: pharmacy was then 'the work of chemists, druggists, apothecaries, grocers and dispensers'.[2] With all these separate outlets for medicines, apprenticeships differed widely. Much of the information concerning the preparation and the dispensing of drugs was vague and unscientific in origin. Many pharmacies were family businesses, where knowledge was passed down from father to son, not regularly subjected to the penetrating gaze and methods of modern scientific practice. The founding members of the new society looked to unify these disparate parts into a recognizable profession established, educated and examined by the society. The title 'pharmacist' was to be validated by the vital influence of the society.

The drugs sold by grocers or apothecaries were of two kinds: patent medicines made off the premises, or medicines concocted in the shop itself. The intricacies of preparation may have been handed down from generation to generation, but much of the substance of this information came from herbals. These ancient books, great composites of botanical and medical wisdom, experience, plagiarism, and fable, were the foundations on which the makers of drugs based their products. From opium to orange peel plants were the key; they were the crude elements of most drugs. (Even now, in the early 21st century, plants provide the active ingredients in 25 per cent of prescription drugs.) However, the fresh and dried leaves, roots, fruit, resins, and bark available to the would-be chemist in Thomas and Daniel's day were no longer confined to those familiar to 17th-century herbalists. As India, the Americas and, most importantly, China, with its sophisticated medical heritage stretching back 2,000 years, became more and more accessible to merchant ships, so increasing numbers of new medicinal plants had been introduced to the market. Botanists, let alone apothecaries, could not keep up. The alien nature of the plant material meant that discerning the quality of the goods and thus the honesty of their brokers was difficult. The adulteration of shipments was common, as was the ignorance of the druggists. A poor appreciation of plants made for bad drugs and bad business. An understanding of botany and a scientific approach to its application to the pharmacist's profession was becoming vital to the development of medicine. It was in this field that Daniel was to acquire an international reputation for intellectual and botanic rigour.

If Clapham provided Daniel with his first lessons in botany, the pharmacy business at Plough Court was to allow his talent for the subject to develop fully. In 1844 he enrolled as a student in the laboratory inside the Pharmaceutical Society's building in Bloomsbury Square. His work at the Plough Court Pharmacy continued, but his part-time studies brought him into the realms of scientific scholarship so suited to his self-possessed powers of analysis. In particular, Jonathan Pereira's lectures on *materia medica* caught Daniel's imagination. These lectures dealt with the botanical sources for drugs, the building blocks from which the pharmacist constructs the product. The inspirational teaching of Pereira set Daniel on the path that was to lead to his great book, *The Pharmacographia*. Daniel lost not only a great tutor but also a good friend when Pereira died at the age of 49 in 1853. It was Daniel who ultimately filled the intellectual gap that

Pereira left and who proved himself a worthy successor.

In a letter to his friend Brenier in 1867 Thomas wrote, in reference to the Exposition Universelle held in Paris that year, that Daniel 'has been appointed Exposition Juror by the British Government he is very scientific and clever, speaks and writes French to perfection and knows many of the savants of Paris.'[3] Thomas loved, respected and was extremely proud of his brother. The slightly arch description of Daniel as being 'very scientific and clever' may well have been penned with a warm smile on Thomas's lips. Thomas understates both Daniel's professional and academic achievements, and the idiosyncratic 'scientific' nature of his personality. Daniel was an exceptional pharmacist and botanist, helping to found the discipline that brought those two subjects together, pharmacognosy. By Daniel's untimely death in 1875 he was judged by many of his peers to lead that field, not only in Britain, but throughout Europe. Part of this reputation rested on *The Pharmacographia*, which Daniel co-authored with Professor Friedrich Fluckiger and which was published in 1874, a few months before Daniel's death from typhoid. This book deals with the commercial, scientific and social 'History of the Principal Drugs of Vegetable Origin Met with in Great Britain and British India'[4]. It was the culmination of his life's work and proved to be a milestone in pharmocognosy.

*The Pharmacographia* is an extremely fine work, bristling with erudition and scholarship, expressed with elegant precision, and much of it the work of Daniel. His contemporaries swiftly acknowledged it to be the standard authority on the subject. In a lecture delivered in 1975, on the centenary of Daniel's death, Professor Edward Shellard declared that: 'there could be little doubt that Daniel Hanbury's contribution was by far the major, since he was concerned with the historical and botanical work necessary to confirm the identity of the drugs'.[5] In his view, *The Pharmacographia*

> certainly enabled pharmacognosy to become an established independent subject of study of major importance and, by establishing the biological sources of the crude drugs in common use, it also gave to pharmacy the status of responsibility, which it so badly needed.[6]

To give some idea of the enormous breadth of scholarship required by Daniel for the compilation of this definitive work, it is worth noting the array of languages in which Daniel had become proficient. As already mentioned, he was fluent in French and could also read German. He had both ancient Greek and Latin, essential for his studies, at his disposal. In addition, Joseph Ince recalls that Daniel also had 'sufficient knowledge of Turkish… [and] some notion of Arabic[, and] …certain Oriental languages and Chinese, besides Spanish and modern Greek, were included in his studies…'[7]

Daniel's reputation was such that by 1867 he had been elected a Fellow of the Royal Society, the Linnaean Society, the Chemical Society and the Royal Microscopical Society. By 1869 he was on the councils of both the Chemical and the Royal Societies. In 1872 he was made an honorary doctor of the University of Munich, a title he was always too modest to assume. He was a member of pharmaceutical societies from Brussels to Argentina. All this was achieved by a man who had left school at the age of 16.

It was botany, rather than languages, that had been Daniel's earliest obsession, and he shared it with, and passed it on to, his brother. As Thomas's eldest brother, separated by nearly seven years, Daniel offered Thomas honest advice and devoted support throughout his life. From their childhood days in Clapham, Daniel nurtured and encouraged Thomas's interest in the natural world.

Botany, scientific endeavour and the industrious assimilation of information suited Daniel's character well. Everything about Daniel was contained and ordered. He hardly ever drank, abhorred tobacco, never ate more than was necessary and always preferred the balance of his plate to be predominately vegetable. He was fearsomely punctual. Any form of ostentation was an anathema to him. His neat appearance, character and manner of dress are said to have remained unchanged from 1850 to his death in 1875. Even his handwriting was eulogized in the obituaries that mourned his passing, as the very model of clarity, regularity and legibility. Fluckiger, for example, enthused:

> All the charm of truth and purity dwelt in his refined, engaging appearance. His exterior, including the expressive firmness and neatness of his handwriting, corresponded harmoniously with the nobility of the soul. He made very high demands on himself in the fulfillment of his duty and in his work, and in this respect he was not lenient towards others, for in his opinion of their proper mode of conduct he gave only the testimony of truth.[8]

Daniel was a slightly-built man, good-looking in a clean, almost plain way, his dark brown hair parted in a line of unwavering straightness. His clothes were of a sober style, of an uncostly dark cloth, and he was always neat. A recognizable stereotype of the scientist is of a bedraggled blur of unkempt hair, pens and spectacles: the 'mad professor' style. Daniel was less a whirlwind of theoretical genius and more an instrument of scientific measurement: well-made, efficient and neatly designed. Nothing about Daniel was spare, everything was functional. Equally, it seems that his social skills were pared down and unencumbered by excess. Ince, a close friend, wrote in another of Daniel's obituary notices:

> A memoir painted *couleur de rose* is an unfaithful thing, and to be despised. It must not be concealed that Daniel Hanbury's avocations and the abstract mould in which the expression of his thoughts were cast inspired a feeling of want of geniality in his more public intercourse with pharmacists. This was alluded to at the time in the following sentence, to which he gave special heed:- 'Personally, we are glad when he is thrown into immediate contact with others of less scientific attainment than himself, for there are some who regret that there should not be a ray more sunshine in his light.' From that date on he steadfastly endeavoured to overcome that apparent chill of mannerism to which attention had been drawn.[9]

Reading the obituary that Ince wrote for his friend, which he later expanded into a short memoir, I was struck by the sense that those who knew Daniel not only accepted his peremptory manner, but loved him for it. This 'apparent chill of mannerism' was a reflection of the transparent nature of the man, his truthfulness, his honesty, his modesty and lack of guile. One of the most revealing elements of the above quotation is Ince's report that, having been criticized for his 'want of geniality', Daniel 'steadfastly endeavoured to overcome' this weakness. Such a task would have been neither easy nor comfortable for the reticent Daniel. His social awkwardness may also shed further light on the difficulties that Thomas experienced in Shanghai society. Both young men, perhaps, were too familiar with the Quaker penchant for truth and honesty to be at ease in general company, where such values might have proved too robust for brittle chatter and light conversation. Ince, in a glorious description of Daniel's scientific papers, captures something of Daniel's style, both as a man and as an author. His works:

> constantly land the investigator a distinct, reliable and practical result. His barque was never showy, nor, though classic, did it ever indulge in painted sails – still less was it swift; but the steersman, quietly self-reliant, made straight for the destined port.[10]

The observation made of Daniel in the *Pharmaceutical Journal*, that 'the discovery or vindication of scientific truth was the ruling passion of his mission in life',[11] is undoubtedly true. Thomas sometimes bemoaned his elder brother's unblinking focus. Ince remarked:

> Better and wiser had it been for him to have carried his bow occasionally unbent, and to have indulged in some degree of relaxation amidst his severer occupations.[12]
>
> To the fascinations of the gay city, even its innocent recreations, he was just as much a stranger as when botanizing at Naples he let Vesuvius continue its irruption without for a moment being diverted from his labours.[13]

All things were viewed through an analytical lens. Life was, perhaps, more digestible if passed through a filter of scientific method. The account of the beagling escapade in China (at the end of Chapter 4) was written by Thomas in a letter to Daniel. Thomas referred to the wildcat killed by the dog as a civet. Daniel's response passed over any amusement at the bizarre scene described to deliver a short dissertation on the differing forms and types of civet, their natural habitats and geographical locations. Daniel's conclusion was that it was highly unlikely to have been a civet. His reply to Thomas closes with a request that, if Thomas happened across another of these cats around Shanghai, he might 'put it into a jar of spirits of wine and address it to Dr Gray, British Museum, London'.[14]

It is easy to paint a portrait of Daniel as an austere, humourless and lonely man, but that would be a false picture. He made and sustained profound friendships, both at home and abroad, counting among his closest friends some of the great botanical and pharmaceutical savants of the period. He was not a cold man, but one who was both thoughtful and generous towards others. His ruling passion for scientific truth may not have endeared him to those at grand social occasions and salons, but it did not extinguish his natural warmth:

> Hanbury had other friends from whose minds his memory will not easily fade – these were little children. For them he had always a smile of welcome and a cheerful word; and in their society he was as unlike a staid and grave philosopher as heart could wish. His way of interesting and amusing them was a sight to see; he never talked down to them but talked them up to him, and yet the children's delight was perfect. At home, and in his study among the varied curiosities and specimens, in the garden showing them rare and beautiful plants, Hanbury was never more charming than when surrounded by a group of children.[15]

Daniel never had children of his own, nor was he destined to leave the family home: as Professor Fluckiger commented in his obituary of Daniel (translated by Katharine Hanbury), 'he had renounced wedded bliss'. Despite this, Daniel had an affinity with children and felt relaxed in their company, helped no doubt by having grown up as the eldest of a large family.

Throughout his childhood and early manhood, until his departure for Shanghai, Thomas always had Daniel near him, as brother, companion and mentor. If one event shows Daniel's influence over Thomas it is most assuredly the trip to the Continent that they undertook in the summer of 1852. The tour lasted for two months, and took in France, Germany, Austria, Switzerland and the Italian lakes. Daniel had begun travelling abroad some years previously, having visited France by 1849. France was to remain a favourite destination of his. He wrote and spoke French fluently, and it was remarked that he underwent a slight transformation when in conversation or correspondence with a French friend or colleague, catching 'something of that charm which characterises the graceful composition of our friends across the sea'.[16] For Thomas, in contrast, this was his first taste of travel and it was to make an impression on him that he would never lose.

The journey was not without a purpose. There was a third member of the party, a friend of Daniel's, a fellow pharmacist and student of *materia medica*. The collection of specimens of crude drugs, pharmaceutical information and practices was the priority. Thomas did his best to help and kept a journal for the family in England. On each arrival at a town or city there developed a pattern. Here, for example, the travellers have arrived in Milan:

> This evening our two Pharmaciens have been to hunt out a wholesale druggists, I did not go as I had so much to write, they returned home laden with things; after staying from 1–2 hours at the place, and seemingly routing out everything it contained, (this is the usual plan when we arrive at a place) altho' they can hardly speak a word of Italian and the people cannot generally understand either French or German, and sometimes not even

the Latin names of their things.[17]

Daniel was unrelenting in his search for material and knowledge, but this demanded purposeful interaction with local people, a habit that Thomas was to emulate. The trip was defined by intellectual curiosity but whether this meant catching butterflies or investigating local customs, this actually allowed for greater involvement with the inhabitants or fellow travellers:

> ...the place where I was filled with Austrians and Italians, who were immensely amused with my butterfly net, one man in particular, would keep jabbering Italian to me, and pressed me very much to take some snuff, which had the appearance of pepper chopped up with a knife, he kept tapping me on the shoulder too, when he saw a white butterfly, for me to get out and catch it, and when I did at last bag a small blue one, there was such a burst of merriment as quite to amuse us even.[18]

> ...we afterwards met a funeral procession to the cemetery proceeding to the cemetery which we followed being curious to see how it was conducted. There was a long procession and a great crowd following after there was not any priest to officiate, but instead a brass band and about twenty women carrying lighted candles four feet long, we were exceedingly shocked and disgusted at the little respect shewn for the dead at the interrment, the coffins (which were merely four rough planks tacked together) being almost thrown in to the graves, and afterwards pelted by a lot of little street boys with stones, the brass band all the while playing merry tunes. D.H. had his pocket handkerchief stolen, which was no more than one could expect in such a rabble.[19]

The tour nourished Thomas's restless desire to leave the humdrum world of the counting house and to travel abroad. It also introduced him to the Italian garden, its structure, form and potential. He describes the garden of Isola Bella on Lake Maggiore, which:

consists of 10 terraces, all more or less ornamental, with statues and vases, and the bottom one with a row of cypress trees; on these terraces not only do the orange, citron, myrtle and pomegranate trees flourish, but also we observed cacti, aloes, two cork trees and a splendid specimen twenty feet high of the camphor tree, and all these surrounded by the clear blue lake, and that again backed by the snowy peaks of the Alps, on one side and the fertile plains of Lombardy on the other... I must say we were rather disappointed in the variety of plants the place afforded, the collection not being nearly equal to Villa Serbelloni on the Lake of Como, tho' there were some individual specimens very curious, such for instance as several different kinds of orange trees from China etc and one of the common kind (a standard) which must have been as tall as the apple tree on our lawn, loaded with fruit and blossom, also some fine opuntias and two specimens of *Chamaerops humilis*, a kind of palm.[20]

The royal 'we' that Thomas uses is not confined to actions such as 'we went to Isola Bella', but is chosen also to express the opinions and responses to the garden: 'we observed' and 'we were disappointed'. Gardens were, perhaps, always a shared experience for Daniel and Thomas. The garden's beautiful situation is duly praised, but some criticism is also levelled at Isola Bella, not for aesthetic reasons, but for a failure to realize its botanic potential. The demand is not for more flowers but for more species. The scientific gardener, the botanist, looks for an array of different species of plant within a garden. The display gardener is concerned with the visual effect of a garden as opposed to content. Even in 1852 the Hanbury brothers perceived a garden as being more than a pleasure ground or a source of fruit and vegetables: for them it was a plant collection.

Thomas's journal of these two months in Europe shows the depth of Daniel's botanic influence and the horticultural shape of things to come. As a pharmacist Daniel perceived the plant world as more than just a horticultural palette. The scientific study of plants and their use by human beings was the subject to which Daniel had committed himself entirely. For him a garden could never be purely ornamental: it must have an intellectual function. A garden should be botanic, containing systematic collections of plant genera and species, correctly catalogued and labelled. Such a garden, for a scholar like Daniel, was a tool, a reference library, a laboratory and an unending tutorial. Under his influence Thomas's achievement of La Mortola became a marriage between the botanic and the beautiful, the public and the private.

The botanic garden was traditionally the preserve of the university, being an exhibition garden in which plant families were regimentally displayed in systematic beds among fine specimen trees. The purpose of such a garden was twofold: the practical instruction of students of botany; and research. At La Mortola this idea of an instructive plant collection was incorporated within a private garden. The garden was a mass of collections, from cacti to dahlias; there was even a systematics garden; but the intention behind their display was aesthetic as well as academic. The Wisley/McAlpine divide of private and public was bridged handsomely at La Mortola.

The scientific focus of the botanic garden has never been purely academic. Economics has always played a major factor in the creation of these plant collections. Research into newly introduced plant species could mean potential new vegetables, fruits, fibres, medicines and trade. Plants that are useful to human beings can be sold for profit. Botanic gardens were thus also the trial grounds for new commodities. The material wealth of the Hanbury family in Clapham was based on the firm of Allen & Hanbury, and the pharmaceutical trade. Plants and their medicinal properties formed the foundation of their livelihood. The Hanbury interest in plants and the family pharmaceutical business were not coincidental.

Another source of inspiration for both Daniel and Thomas has found its expression in botanic gardens. The first appearance of botanic gardens, in Italy during the 16th century, occurred simultaneously with the arrival of botanic discoveries from the New World. The development of European botanic gardens is entwined in the history of colonial expansion, but they have roots in theology as well as in economic botany. Scholars and academics hoped that the great American continents would prove to be exhibitions of the previously concealed wonders of God's creation. They earnestly wished that the human discovery of the Americas might turn out to be a tool of divine revelation. There was a belief that the study of plants from these new lands might lead to a greater understanding of God Himself. The early European botanic gardens offered a potential glimpse of the Kingdom of Heaven.

The plant world serving as a means of becoming closer to God was an attractive and liberating concept, and it was not limited simply to exotic flora. Ralph Austen, for example, in his book *A Treatise of Fruit Trees* (1653), concerned himself primarily with orchards of apple and pear trees, but he also captures concisely the essence of this theory:

The World is a great Library, and Fruit trees are some of the Bookes wherein we may read & see plainly the Attributes of God, his Power, Wisdome, Goodnesse...The botanic garden was understood by some to be a catalogue of divinity. Plants that were of benefit to human beings were construed as further manifestations of God's munificence. Medicinal plants, in particular, figured highly in such interpretations of the natural world. The Scriptures themselves declare, in Ecclesiasticus (38:4):'The Lord hath created Medicines out of the Earth and he that is wise will not abhor them.'

The appearance of Charles Darwin's *The Origin of Species* (1859) had proved that the study of the natural world would not always meet with the approval of theologians and priests. Although it challenged the established biblical orthodoxy, Darwin's work could be seen in some ways to have made even more poignant the links between botanic research and matters of religious belief.

The Hanbury family's Quaker faith was profound and Daniel was no exception to this. Daniel's religious beliefs and their importance to him is made evident by his close friend and colleague, Fluckiger:

It is due to the fine character of Daniel Hanbury to reveal the source of his unbroken equanimity – a deep spirit of devotion which found its expression, not in outward declarations, but in the uniform tenor of his life. Sometimes, indeed, the angel troubled the waters, and he was not afraid to give utterance to the deep sentiments of his heart – once more especially, when he contended for the spirituality and the vital influence of the communion of which he was a member.[21]

The garden was more than a scientific, economic or ornamental exercise. The Quaker faith of the Hanburys provided a deep sense of respect and awe for the natural world. The garden was a place of spirituality as well.

There is an ancient, slouching gateway that leads from the northern terrace of the Palazzo Orengo out into the garden. Here the path naturally takes the visitor into the Topia, a long, elegantly arching pergola, shrouded in a mix of climbers and creepers, from the Banksian Rose at one end to the exotic *Solandra maxima* at the other. At the end of this shady walk is the eastern boundary of the garden. The view is striking, stretching across the bay to the shores of Ventimiglia and Bordighera. It is a charming place to sit, and was a favourite spot for Thomas and Katharine. Carved in stone, by the Topia's end, are these words from the Latin text of Genesis 3:8: '*Audiverunt vocem Domini Dei deambulantis in horto*' ('They heard the voice of the Lord God walking in the garden'). For both Thomas and Daniel Hanbury a botanic garden was a heady mixture of the mind, the wallet and the soul.

Daniel's friendship with the illustrious Hooker family began in the 1850s and that decade saw his co-authorship of the Admiralty's *Manual of Botany* with William Hooker. It was with William's son Joseph Hooker, who was to succeed his father as Director of Kew in 1865, that Daniel cemented the links between the Hanburys and Kew. In the autumn of 1860 Daniel and Joseph Hooker set off on a two-month plant-collecting trip to the Holy Land, taking in what is now Lebanon, Syria, Palestine and Israel. These nations cover an area of enormous botanical wealth, and it is a richness mirrored by the economic and medicinal value of many of its species. Inevitably, this extraordinary flora is now diminishing rapidly, as its habitats are overwhelmed by the demands of agriculture and housing. It is an area currently targeted by Kew and the Millennium Seed Bank as one of great importance under great threat. For Daniel it was a botanic fiesta, but the trip also brought a not unwelcome release from the drudgery of the pharmacy business and Plough Court. Daniel had been an enthusiastic traveller in Europe, but these two months were to be among the most challenging of his life.

Then as now, the inhabitants of the Holy Land often expressed their religious loyalties in acts of merciless violence. The report of their entry in to Damascus reads:

> Great alarm prevailed amongst the Christians, who were all leaving after the massacre, and ruins piled four feet deep were in every lane; there were heaps of mutilated corpses, bones and stench; burnt books and pictures; 3,500 to 4,000 troops; much sickness, dysentery and diarrhoea.[22]

Witnessing these scenes of terrible cruelty and suffering can only have had a profound effect on Daniel. In 1853 Thomas had complained of Daniel's indefatigable work ethic and had wished that Daniel would:

> take a good holiday, it is such a mistake and pity to tye oneself so much to business, and altho he says he does not need it on the grounds of health, yet even in that case it is quite proper to take one, if it were only for the sake of enlarging one's ideas and seeing something of the world…[23]

The horrors of Damascus were not constituents of 'a good holiday', but the description of the human wreckage with which the city was strewn might easily be mistaken for a fragment of Thomas's correspondence from China. Thomas was to find, on his return to England in 1866, that nobody in the Hanbury family or among their

Clapham friends was interested in, or could relate to, his experiences in China except Daniel. Only Daniel would have had any conception of the national tragedy that Thomas had lived through. If Thomas were to talk to anyone on these matters it would have been Daniel.

Their correspondence, though it was often dominated by plants, was by no means exclusively so. Daniel gave Thomas much needed support and encouragement during his trouble with William Crampton, and appreciated the risks of the new partnership. Daniel also believed very strongly in the worth of Thomas's learning Chinese and nurturing good relations with Chinese people:

I think it is of great importance that there is at least one European who befriends the Chinese and is willing to hear their troubles and accord them assistance in their difficulties; and I do not regret thy having to put aside more agreeable occupations in order to be thus useful.[24]

Within the family Daniel provided Thomas with a dependable and independent ally, in a way that no one else could. Daniel's bachelor status played a large part in this. Thomas was close to their sister, Anna, but once she had married and had children their letters, though no less affectionate, were certainly less frequent. The similarities and close relationship between Thomas and Daniel also serve to highlight how different they were from their other brothers.

Sampson, older than Thomas, had moved to Cornwall in the early 1850s to try his hand at farming. The move had been perplexing for the rest of the family, and had ended in failure and large financial losses for Sampson and his wife. Capel was rather bolder in his social habits than the previous Hanbury children. As a youth he habitually came home late at night, refusing to explain why to his parents or to

Daniel. Things failed to improve after his marriage. In a letter to Thomas dated 27 October 1870 Daniel despaired of Capel's behaviour. Capel left his home in Tooting to travel to the Netherlands, where he took a shooting lodge with some friends. Waiting eagerly for his return were several local tradesmen, clutching unpaid bills, but also his poor wife and children. When their father, Daniel Bell Hanbury, died in 1882 Capel's share of the inheritance had two thousand pounds plus interest deducted for money owing to the deceased. This was most certainly not the Hanbury way.

Daniel and Thomas' fierce intellects were never going to be replicated by the entire family, and Barclay Hanbury served as living testament to the lottery of genetics. In a letter to Daniel of 22 November 1865 Thomas wrote, with morose resignation: 'Barclay I find has not learned to spell correctly yet and I suppose he never will.[25] The unfortunate Barclay may have been dyslexic, but in the 19th century, of course, dyslexia was as yet an undiscovered condition. Whatever the cause, even Daniel had to admit that Barclay was a hopeless case.[26]

Within the family, then, Daniel and Thomas were equals in their relative success, sharing a determined and disciplined approach to life. Daniel was Thomas's confidant and some remarks in their letters were regularly prefaced with a warning about confidentiality. Daniel was in the habit of reading Thomas's letters to his parents and such measures were vital to prevent anxiety. Thomas often encouraged Daniel to invest in his Shanghai schemes, as he did with all his family. Occasionally, however, opportunities were offered to Daniel alone. These are not signs of conspiratorial behaviour but, in a family founded on truth and transparency, their allegiance and complicity were significant.

Daniel remained in the family firm for 29 years, retiring in 1870.

As he wrote to a fellow botanist and plant collector, Dr Richard Spruce, on 29 September that year: 'I look forward with great pleasure to freedom from a good deal of wearing, but not always disagreeable occupation.'[27] During those 29 years at Plough Court Daniel had compromised aspects of his scientific pursuits for the sake of business. His retirement was to see no relaxation of his 'unflinching diligence', not least because the period saw him complete his share of the work on *The Pharmacographia*.

Daniel's withdrawal from the pharmaceutical trade also contributed to his being able to exert a tremendous and lasting influence on the garden at La Mortola. The proud and critical Ludwig Winter, La Mortola's head gardener from 1869 to 1875, had no doubts as to the quality of Daniel's horticultural abilities. In a letter to Daniel he wrote, in his indomitable style:

Your suggestions for a characteristic arrangement of Your Brother's Garden and Your contribution of interesting plants etc are so highly valuable that one is longing for your personal assistance when the time of planting arrives.[28]

Not only did Daniel have a vast wealth of botanical and horticultural knowledge, obviously far superior to Thomas's, but he had access to a global network of botanists and botanical gardens. It was largely through this network that the celebrated plant collection at La Mortola was garnered. The respectful and affectionate relationship cherished by Thomas and Daniel was to be the most vital and creative of foundations for the garden. The Giardini Hanbury was begun in 1867: for nearly two and a half years, from June 1869 until November 1871, Daniel oversaw the management of the garden and forged the template of its future.

# Chapter Seven
# A garden in Italy

'I like my property here the more I see of it and am extremely well satisfied to have purchased. My eldest Brother has spent a week here with me, but I am now quite alone surrounded by a population of Italian peasants whose language I am (not very successfully) endeavouring to acquire. I have two rooms in a cottage on the side of the hill among the olive trees, and am day by day actively engaged superintending the alterations and embellishments of my Palazzo Orengo, which when completed will make it much finer than it ever was... I have not yet purchased the title, nor have I found any suitable Italian countess to marry but you can live in hopes of hearing of these events some day – As to going back to Shanghai this autumn I begin to falter not seeing that I can do much good when I get there. I must make up my mind in August or September but I fancy you will not see me.'[1]

This passage from Thomas's letter to Iveson, his friend and some-time business partner or agent, written in July 1867, serves as an excellent illustration of the new and happy sense of purpose that he had discovered at La Mortola. Shanghai had little to offer Thomas in comparison to the excitement of his new property in Italy.

His health was still not sufficiently recovered, however. A month earlier, in a letter to his friend Brenier, Thomas had complained of suffering from torpor of the liver and, although the renaissance of his spirits continued, he was clearly unenthused by the prospect of a return to China. Thomas relished overseeing the repairs and renovations to the palazzo, but demands of family and business meant that his time was divided between England and Italy. Bourrit & Simmler looked after his building interests while he was away, but developing the garden presented a challenge of its own. Daniel's advice and help had proved invaluable already, but the partnership of Thomas and Daniel was not going to be sufficient to renew the fortunes of the garden.

'Work in the Garden at Murtola to be carried out by Mr Antonio Lorenzi during the absence of Thomas Hanbury. Murtola 13 May 1867': so begins the very first list of instructions issued by Thomas for the construction and management of his garden at La Mortola. It is not a document of vast horticultural importance, concerning itself with the tending of the fruit trees and their crops, the weeding and the digging. The first five underlined headings run: '<u>Labourers to be employed</u> ... <u>The Tanks</u> ... <u>Watering the Garden</u> ... <u>Manuring the Fruit-trees</u>' and '<u>The Fruit</u>'. Its significance and interest lies most obviously in its very form. Such written instructions became the standard format for the management of the garden for many years to come. Thomas was not going to be in permanent residence and such documents were to be the evidence, not just of his absences from La Mortola, but also of his sense of the need for control. This list is also of interest because of the three subjects on which it concentrates: fruit, water and staff. For me at least, Thomas Hanbury's garden can be defined by these three elements. The garden was always at heart a productive entity, whether the produce be lemons, seeds or knowledge. The struggle for water in cultivating the garden was the focus of all of the problems of climate and location that determined the nature of the garden at La Mortola. The relationships among all those who managed and tended the garden, and their responses to the garden itself, were the catalysts that turned the water into fruit.

The first of these challenges to face Thomas was simply to find some staff. Lorenzi had more or less presented himself to Thomas as his local factor or foreman at the first opportunity. Thomas, with no standard Italian, let alone local dialect, at his disposal, was left with little choice but to accept his services. The immediate task set out for Lorenzi was 'Labourers to be employed'. These labourers were to consist of three or four men and five or six women, who were to begin the process of reclaiming the garden from its state of decay, and to set about securing the water supply and storage for the garden. However, it soon became clear to Thomas that the rigours of transforming the rocky terraces and hillside of La Mortola into a garden were going to need more than the attentions of labourers, vaguely supervised by the indolent Lorenzi. By 1868 Thomas had realized that he would have to employ a head gardener.

In 1868 the garden at La Mortola may have been suffering from years of under-nourishment and neglect but, with the arrival of Thomas and Daniel, a deficit of strong personality was not one of the garden's faults. The appointment of Ludwig Winter to the post of head gardener introduced another powerful personality, and the third and final element of the triumvirate that was to nurture and develop the garden in its crucial early years, 1868–75. Winter was a young man of 22 when he moved to La Mortola. His horticultural career had begun in a nursery at Erfurt and had seen him study botany at Potsdam, and then work in Heidelberg and Bonn as a landscape architect. He was a good draughtsman and artist, and had been employed in Paris making botanical drawings. He had gone to Paris to work on the International Botanical Exhibition, but following this he had found work at the Royal Gardens of the Tuileries. His stay there was brief, however. It is said that he was dismissed on the spot when he was heard whistling 'La Marseillaise' in the presence of the Empress Eugènie. This story may, perhaps, be apocryphal, but that it achieved some sort of credibility says a great deal of Winter's character and his attitude to authority. From Paris he moved to Hyères and it was from there that he moved to La Mortola, on the recommendation of the Huber nursery. The earliest photograph of Winter shows the pale and plain features of his bespectacled face lost among a prodigious growth of untamed hair and beard. Winter was of a slim enough build to cause Thomas some anxiety as to his ability to carry out some of the more physically taxing tasks that the job demanded. Yet within this unprepossessing exterior was a character of passion and determination.

The plans for La Mortola were complicated by the unavoidable necessity of Thomas's return to China, accompanied by his wife. They were to be absent from the Palazzo Orengo and its garden for nearly two and a half years. Thomas and Katharine's voyage to China, via the United States, began in June 1869 and saw them arrive in Shanghai on 8 December: 'We enjoyed our travel in the States very much and were even able to laugh at the rampant democratic ideas prevalent in the cars which rather takes the silvering off the 'silver palace cars'. I allude to such things as 25 ladies and gentlemen using one hair brush belonging to the company, however we survived the sight of such things.'[2]

As we have seen, Winter's early interest in democracy had been demonstrated in his liking for revolutionary anthems. His natural antipathy for authority became a familiar cause of friction. With Thomas thousands of miles away, Daniel was responsible for both house and garden, with the assistance of Lorenzi and Winter respectively. In reply to one of his brother's early reports Thomas wrote to him on 14 January 1870:

I judge from your remarks that everything goes on as it used to. Winter takes an interest and pride in the place but is rather more obstinate than the most obstinate mule; the same want of rain and moisture afflicts the place but strange to say the plants do not die from the drought. Lorenzi luxuriates in idleness but keeps faithful to my interests.

The relationship between Winter and the Hanburys was sometimes fraught, particularly in the first three years. Friction between head gardeners and their employers is not uncommon, and it is a problem of which all garden owners should be aware. An employer naturally wants to have the very best head gardener possible working in their garden. These tend to be enthusiastic, imaginative and knowledgeable people, driven by a genuine love for gardens and plants. The trouble with appointing someone of this calibre to take charge of your garden is that they are bound have strong opinions concerning the design and running of it. They may quickly forget that it is you, not they, who owns the garden and may never miss an opportunity to pour professional scorn on what they perceive to be your amateur attempts at horticultural *savoir-faire*. The rule is not to employ a chef if it is a *plongeur* that you require. Winter was very much a chef and he took any criticism of his craft poorly.

Winter's abilities as a capable landscaper of the gardens were evident from the very beginning of his employment. Within a few months he had suggested the removal of several olive trees from around the palazzo, renovated the Topia and improved the path down to the palazzo by adding gentle curves to its steep gradient. All of these changes were appreciated and approved of by Thomas. Winter's dealings with people, however, were often greeted with rather less enthusiasm. In his light-hearted complaint to Daniel, of 2 September 1872, about visitors' tipping him, Winter, perhaps bridled by their condescension, was under no illusion as to the bluntness of his style:

I very much detest this custom and was sometimes offended here when people would reward me for a little act of politeness by money, which of course, I refused with german coarseness.[3]

Winter's social graces lacked a certain finesse, and often negated the positive effects of his skill and achievements. Daniel kept in regular contact with Thomas and it is evident that Winter's personality brought him into conflict with his superiors:

Winter has been obliging and exertive – sometimes however reminding me of the son in the parable who said 'I will not' but went.[4]

Winter told me he had a notion of some day starting a seed-growing establishment in the Nervia Valley. I was not sorry to hear it, as it may offer a way for a change of gardeners which would be no bad move. W. has been rather offended and sulky the last few days because I would not consent to the pulling down of a stone buttress on the south side of the large tank.[5]

To an undemonstrative man of unimpeachably high standards such as Daniel was, Winter's petulance must have seemed absurd and childishly unprofessional.

In Winter's defence it can be pointed out that he did not have an easy job. The members of his workforce were agricultural labourers, erratic in their habits and thoroughly unmotivated. He was expected to oversee and work with them, while also bringing on seedlings, cuttings and young plants in his makeshift nursery. In the summer months simply keeping the plants watered and alive must have taken up most of his time. There are few times in the life of a large garden that will match this embryonic stage for demands on its gardeners. As land was cleared and new beds dug, so the areas requiring maintenance and weeding increased. Fragile young plants populated the garden, and were highly vulnerable to animal damage, solar radiation, drought and disease. Winter's responsibilities included the vegetable garden and orchards, the produce from which was sold in Ventimiglia or sent to Clapham or Shanghai. He was also expected to maintain all the plant records and labels, as well as show round any visitors who happened to drop by. Communication with his superiors was not straightforward, and hence clarity about the balance of responsibility was not simple to establish. The chain of command was extended, with Thomas thousands of miles away in China and Daniel, the caretaker manager, living in Clapham.

Ludwig Winter's cause was not helped by Sebastiano Lorenzi, the Hanburys' foreman from the very beginning, who was lazy and dishonest. Both Thomas and Daniel felt that his integrity was questionable, and, perhaps by association, the reputation of his colleague Winter was also besmirched. Thomas wrote to Daniel from Shanghai on 14 January 1870:

I am glad that the kitchen garden is in a better state, I attribute its betterness however to the fact that Lorenzi and Winter have a direct interest in making it produce well and therefore I do not gather the consolation I otherwise should in believing that an adequate show is being made by Winter for the money I spend at La Mortola.

Lorenzi was meant to be helping Winter organize the workforce, but he seldom left the comfort of the kitchen when the Hanburys were away. As a result Winter's job was made impossibly difficult; yet his silence suggests that he felt too compromised to broach the subject with Daniel or Thomas. Daniel's suspicions of Lorenzi grew nonetheless. He reported them to Thomas, adding: 'Winter, I think, is quite honest and good-principled, whatever he may not be.'[6]

At the end of 1871, following Thomas's return to La Mortola, tensions were brought to a head. Thomas became increasingly aware that Winter was an honest and hard-working employee, struggling in difficult circumstances. This excerpt from a letter that Thomas wrote to Iveson illustrates Winter's enthusiasm and the satisfaction of his employer with the healthy plant collection at La Mortola:

I hope you have shipped the Cycas Palms as I have requested before leaving. My German gardener here is quite in a state of excitement in view of the prospect of receiving them. Nearly all the rare plants that my brother + myself have collected from various parts of the world are thriving capitally, and I have already a most valuable collection, the envy of many a botanist.[7]

In December 1871 Thomas and Winter exchanged a series of letters concerning Winter's future, which resulted in an important change in their relationship. From this period onwards the relationships that Winter had with Thomas and Daniel developed into mutual respect, mutual trust and even friendship. Thomas, with the confidence given by being in residence once more, allowed Winter greater freedom and responsibility, and Winter repaid his trust in kind. Thomas had finally seen Lorenzi for the duplicitous sloth that he was. Lorenzi had stolen some wine out of the palazzo's cellars and had attempted to pass them discreetly through the household accounts. An attempt to conceal such activity from Thomas Hanbury in an account book, of all things, was an act of gross stupidity. On 29 December 1871 Thomas initially wrote Lorenzi a stinging letter, sacking him. Thomas relented, however, crossing out his first draft and sending Lorenzi this letter instead:

> The account of wine I do not find correct as both my brother and myself are sure that we did not consume 26 bottles when we were last at Mortola... I must tell you frankly I am not satisfied with the very small amount of work you do for me while I am away from Mortola. I find the men who are employed on the property become very lazy because it is impossible for Mr. Winter to be constantly looking after them and attending to other parts of the garden. Formerly you were accustomed to see that the men laboured constantly and did not waste their time, now it appears to me you remain in the kitchen or go about your own affairs and consider it is none of your business. Thus it will be necessary for me to engage an under-gardener to keep the men up to work, which you could perfectly well do if you exerted yourself properly. I am determined to change the present system and to require full work from all to whom I pay wages.

The pastoral idyll of Thomas's early days at La Mortola was inevitably supplanted by a more mundane, and occasionally trying, reality. The improved relationship between Winter and Thomas was an important factor in bridging the gap that lay between the Palazzo Orengo and the villages that surrounded it. The people of La Mortola had always been most grateful to Thomas and appreciative of his efforts. After his arrival at La Mortola on 25 September 1867 Thomas had reported to Katharine:

> I had sent a telegram from Toulon in the morning to announce my coming; through some negligence, however, it had not been delivered 'til half an hour before I arrived; nevertheless, the village was all astir, and I receive the most enthusiastic greeting: windows were illuminated, little bonfires made among the olive trees lit up the road, and a crowd of twenty or thirty men and women bearing English and Italian flags escorted me to the humble cottage I occupy on the side of the hill above the Palazzo.

When Thomas arrived in La Mortola with his father, in 1868, the whole village had turned out to bid them welcome and '…my father was quite affected to tears with these manifestations'.

Thomas's generosity was recognized but his arrival at La Mortola brought with it some abrupt changes to local habits and customs:

> Whitting [Mrs Hanbury's English maid] came in the greatest state of alarm the other evening to report that there were two objects in white in the garden, with hideous white faces, and that they were dancing about! It turned out that they were two of the villagers dressed in white, and with masks, and that it is some old custom that permits this. Afterwards two others came, and I chased them away.[8]

Some changes intruded more noticeably into the lives of the villagers, the Mortolati. Thomas wanted most of the garden to be heavily cultivated and planted, but he wished to return the Vallone, the gully that followed the stream to the sea, to some approximation of a natural habitat. The hillside had been stripped bare by generations of local people searching for firewood and any seedlings were devoured by goats. Thomas restricted access to his land, banning the collection of firewood. Just as controversial for many of the Mortolati was a ban on shooting birds anywhere on Thomas's estate. Many Italians still regard it as their unassailable right to shoot any feathered creature that is foolish enough to come into range. The fact that the garden at La Mortola was utterly bereft of any birds would have appeared to many locals less as a source of ecological anxiety and more as a proud testament to the straight-shooting skills of La Mortola's menfolk. So determined was Thomas to restore bird life to his garden, however, that in 1878 the garden accounts registered payment for 16 kilograms of bird food. Such acts of eccentric extravagance must have caused some amused and perplexed head-shaking among his Italian employees.

Liguria is characterized by the steep and stony hillsides that furrow its topography, and nothing is more Ligurian about these hillsides than the contoured grey lines of stone terraces that run from slope to slope across the region. The precipitous land may appear, at first glance, to defy agriculture, but hundreds of years of bloody-minded devotion to the olive has left a dry-stone human fingerprint embossed on much of the landscape. Travel up and away from the coast to small towns and villages, such as the aptly named Olivetta, and one can walk for an hour along the banks of the local river and still see the crumbling mini-aqueducts that once drew water to inaccessible terraces. The investment of time and huge physical effort in such a project is staggering. I have written of the importance of the olive already (in Chapter 1), but the following passage from Dr J.H. Bennet's *Winter and Spring on the Shores of the Mediterranean* (1875) is worth quoting, as it captures succinctly the human significance of the olive terrace:

> These terraces are very expensive to make – as much so, I have been told, as houses; whereas the product is prospective only. The man who builds them sinks his capital more for his children's benefit than for his own… If he plants Olive trees, they grow so slowly, that even in twenty years the produce is insignificant. The stones, even, have to crumble into the soil, under the influence of moisture, wind and weather…
>
> And yet the mountain-sides are scarred with these terraces, which rise in successive tiers, and are the foundation of the agricultural riches of the country. They are the evidence, in stone, of the thrift and industry of past generations – a silent but eloquent monument of the domestic virtues of the forefathers of the present race. Many new terraces have been built during the last few years, owing to the increasing prosperity of the inhabitants.[9]

Thomas kept many of the olive trees that had lived on his property for hundreds of years, but a great number were destroyed for the making of new beds and the opening up of views. For his agriculturally based workforce it must have been an unholy and disheartening business. Cultivation for food or profit was rational employment and those elements of Thomas's garden flourished. Creating a botanic garden that involved the removal of hundreds of years of ancestral husbandry must have appeared cruel lunacy to some of the poor subsistence farmers of La Mortola. Such cultural differences may have fuelled the occasional infantile incident. Winter wrote to Thomas about such vandalism on 18 December 1871:

> I wrote to you yesterday in hurry and under great indignation, which overcame me, when I found on my ordinary Sunday morning round various trees in your property spoiled by impudent hands and ordure put in many places with evident bad intention.[10]

Winter added that 'the Priest tells me that his reproaches in the school are met with shrugs'. Thomas, to his credit, took a disappointed but relaxed view of the affair. Events such as this were rare and Winter's role as liaison between Thomas and his employees developed with the improvement in their own relationship. In 1870 Winter had married a local girl. If he ever had felt separated from the local community, that distance may now have been lessened by some degree. With Thomas resident once again at La Mortola from the autumn of 1871, difficulties and disputes could be discussed, and settled, with much more ease.

The motivation of the staff was the primary hurdle that Winter had to overcome. On 7 January 1872 he wrote to Thomas, less than a month after the vandalism incident:

> I much have thought about a practical manner to introduce more voluntary sense of duty into the minds of your labourers – without which a man will always remain a mere indifferent instrument and I believe that severity should always be assisted with benevolence; sincere affection and gratitude will be their products from which the best fruits will spontaneously result, without forcing.

A very benevolent act it would be on your side if you could augment the daily wage of the men one *sous* a day and keep this *sous* in cash, the amount of which would serve for supporting the people in eventual sickness that affords the treatment of a physician and in a later time for a pension of those, which are getting old. If any labourer does not answer (obstinately) to his duties, he would be sent off and lose his part of this communal fund. Those of your labourers having no other pecuniary gain must live indeed very poorly.

Batschi for instance gains about 40 francs (in average) per month in your property – his wife in average 16 francs – together 56 Francs; they must pay 22 Francs per month to the nurse of their child – are remaining 34 francs for all costs of life for two persons. You see that is indeed very little and you will not be wondered more, that Batschi is got much older in a few years, particularly as he is one of those that aim to do their duty by truly working.[11]

Thomas's reply four days later was very much in sympathy with Winter's suggestions:

I think your ideas are very good and when I visit Mortola as I hope to do at the end of next month I shall further discuss the matter with you and see if the arrangement can be made. I was very sorry to see Batchi looking so much older when we returned from China…

With Lorenzi deemed untrustworthy, Winter had become the main source of local information during Thomas's trips to London. Staff problems and wages were common subjects of their correspondence. Thomas kept a firm hand on the cash box; Winter cared about those he oversaw, but he also defended Thomas's interests. In 1873 these matters ripened into militancy:

> The attempt of striking of your men finished as miserably as I expected. I remonstrated how stupid and unfair their behaviour was, leaving so coarse an alternative to their employer. That you did not promise them any augmentation of wages at present but you would take their conditions in consideration when you return. Anyone who would like to go – might go! The effect was that none went off – that one would lay the charge at the other – none would be guilty – all innocent and I must use all my authority to prevent a general cudgelling between them.[12]

Thomas, though generous in charity and in kindness, was not a believer in weighty pay packets. Letters from Shanghai to La Mortola are dotted with references to what Thomas would have thought as 'competitive' wages. He retained this concern into his later years. For example, in 1900 he made his second son, Daniel (born in 1876) his secretary, and manager of the considerable Hanbury interests in Ventimiglia, Bordighera and Alassio. After Daniel's first year in post Thomas had to bow to his son's appeals for better remuneration. Clearly Thomas made no exceptions, even for his own son, when it came to money and his employees.

To take another example: Alwin Berger, Curator of the gardens from 1897 to 1914, was, perhaps, the most gifted botanist that La Mortola has ever enjoyed as a member of staff. His area of greatest expertise was in succulent plants, of which La Mortola's collection was then one of the finest in the world. Succulents were also Thomas's favourites. Berger published a series of books on various genera of succulents. To give an indication of Berger's professional standing and reputation, the following was written in 1950 by G.W. Reynolds, once maestro of all things Aloe: 'Berger's monograph of the genus Aloe is a work of outstanding merit, and has been the standard Aloe work of reference since it was published in 1908.' It is hard to imagine a better person to curate Thomas's garden, but so meagre were Berger's wages that in 1902 he threatened to leave La Mortola unless Thomas doubled his pay.

The gardens of La Mortola were not an isolated hotbed of political foment. The gardeners were following a national trend, even if they lacked any notion of solidarity. Industrial action had become an increasingly common mode of dissent in Italy. The year 1872 had seen 25 separate large-scale strikes, which were unprecedented events in Italy. These strikes were urban in the main and Turin, for example, spent nine days stultified by strike action. The Associazione fra gli Opera Tipografici Italiani (Association of Italian Typographical Workers), founded as 1872 drew to a close, was Italy's first national trade union. It led a two-month strike in the following year. In 1873 the number of strikes intensified to 103, a figure unsurpassed until 1889. Italian workers were becoming familiar with the notion of a strike. La Mortola was a part of emergent Italy and as such was not immune to the trials that afflicted the nation.[13]

The withdrawals of labour from the garden that confronted Winter were not limited to strike action. The treaty between Italy and France, which had seen Nizza become Nice, had placed an international border across traditional routes to markets. For the Italian population of La Mortola the nearest town, Mentone/Menton, was now in another country. Smuggling became a generally accepted means by which business might be carried on as usual and as a way to earn good money. On 25 August 1873 Winter wrote to Thomas to tell him 'I am now seriously concerned with a question of some importance for your property', for six of the 11 men in Thomas's employment in the garden at La Mortola were seriously involved in smuggling:

> As far as their journeys were of short duration I did not make severe objection to it, but now as they are undertaking voyages of eight to ten days I consider the matter as intolerable for the interests of your estate... the demoralising effect of irregular life which will destroy all discipline I had care to maintain which I think is the soul of all regulated labour.[14]

Some of the smugglers had proved to be good, relatively knowledgeable and previously loyal employees, and the group represented over half of Winter's male workforce. Winter gave them an ultimatum: 'Abandon the smuggling or abandon the service of Mr Hanbury.' In October five men were sacked as a result of their continued criminal absence. Winter looked to the village of Latte for replacements, but such an upset to the garden staff further demonstrates the tribulations of Winter's position, as he tried to compromise between flexibility and firm discipline.

Winter's own attitude to the actual illegality of the smuggling was extremely relaxed. On 25 November 1873 Winter wrote to Thomas concerning the arrival of a chest of tea from London at Menton. The customs officers on the border were fastidious:

> Tea is subjected to an extremely high duty in Italy (I hear 50% of the value) we shall however avoid the heavy charge passing it with the boat; there is hardly any risk.[15]

The duty on tea must have seemed punitive to the British community in Italy. There was a duty of 100 francs on every 100 kilograms of tea, while 100 kilograms of coffee could be imported at the cost of a mere five francs. The duty paid even for 100 kilograms of gunpowder was only 12 francs.[16]

The trade disputes and rivalries between Italy and France could make life extremely difficult for Thomas and his garden. Border tensions between the two countries could result in minor inconveniences, or in serious annoyance. Thomas wrote to his friend Sir William Thistleton-Dyer in April 1879:

The first Mentone Horticultural & Agricultural Exposition takes place tomorrow. I cannot exhibit much, as in addition to the Italian law which would prevent my plants from coming back to the garden, the French have just enacted a revengeful ordinance to prevent anything in the shape of a plant with roots from entering their country if coming from Italy.[17]

Fifteen and a half years later, in October 1894, he wrote, again to Thistleton-Dyer:

Cordiality does not increase between the French and Italians + unfortunately, I am an innocent victim of their ill-humour.

We can no longer drive into Mentone! the new regulations being that all animals must be presented before the French Veterinary at Ventimiglia who gives a health certificate 'good for 24 hours'; as the procurement of this precious document means 4 miles to Ventimiglia and 4 back before beginning to start for Mentone of course it is the equivalent of a ban.[18]

Thomas himself, like Winter, was quite capable of flouting the law when it came to his beloved plants, especially if they were being sent from Kew:

I must now thank you most sincerely for the truly magnificent lot of plants you have sent, which arrived the day before yesterday in the most satisfactory and perfect condition, thanks to the excellent packing.

...to elude the vigilance of the Custom House officers at the Italian frontier the poor plants had to be repacked in Mentone into a barrel which was covered with sacking & passed off as a sack of cement on a *charette* laden with that commodity, but actually only one plant was injured and the rest looked as fresh as possible.[19]

The Italian officials' obsession with plant material was the result of the devastating effects of a tiny, sap-sucking Californian insect, *Phylloxera*. This creature was the nemesis of the European grape vine. It had been introduced through the importation of American vines for grafting purposes between 1858 and 1863. Whatever the process of its arrival, it was to be found in England by 1863 and shortly afterwards in France. At the height of its menace *Phylloxera* was responsible for the destruction of some two and a half million acres of vineyards, at an annual cost of £50 million, and these figures are for France alone. Italy was understandably anxious to keep its vines free of this terrible pest. It was to prove an impossible task. The entry for 16 August 1884 in Thomas's diary reads: 'Government *phylloxera* commission visited Mortola and detected five vines attacked in the Scario vineyard. Ordered 50 square metres to be destroyed.'

The duties and red tape that entangled all those who passed between Italy and France were far from being the products of the *phylloxera* threat alone. They represented the long-running rivalry, even enmity, between the governments of both nations. Having removed the Papacy from the government of Rome and greatly reduced its political power nationally, Italy was suspicious of France as the leading European defender of Catholicism. For those who shared the new Italian sense of nationhood republican France made for an uneasy neighbour in Europe, while colonial France made for a powerful competitor in the western Mediterranean and North Africa. In 1882 Italy signed the Triple Alliance with Austria–Hungary and Germany for mutual protection in the event of a French attack. The 'tariff war' that then broke out between the two countries, in 1888, was the result of Italy's protectionist tariffs, which targeted French imports, while making concessions to those of Austria–Hungary. The result was a fall in exports from Italy to France, which dropped from 41 per cent of all Italian exports to a mere 18 per cent. Two thirds of this market loss could not be recovered elsewhere. The Italian wine growers, now feeling the effects of the dreaded *Phylloxera*, were devastated by plummeting demand and prices. Where exports had been around 2.25 million hectolitres per annum in the mid-1880s, by 1890 they were below one million hectolitres. Olive-growers were to find their trade equally damaged. Particularly in Italy's southern regions, entire areas of economic activity were wiped out.[20]

The specific national tensions around Nice and Savoy could be expected to bubble up around La Mortola and Mentone every now and then, but, for the most part, the local people endeavoured to circumvent the obstacles that international politics cast before them. The fragility of relations was sometimes exposed, however, as is evident in Gustave Cronomeyer's report to Thomas, dated 4 October 1891:

Today is the inauguration festival of the Garibaldi Monument in Nizzo. Much people had driven these days from Italy for Nice for partaking in that solemnity. I am very much on tiptoe to hear of the success of that festival. For, as you may have already read, at Rome at the second October French pilgrims – priests have insulted in a very absurd manner the tomb of King Victor Emmanuel, one of them has been sprinkling upon the tomb and others had cried out abusing words. The 'Secolo XIX' of yesterday brought long columns on the commotion and excitement of the Roman people. I think this accident happened just in a wrong and unfortunate moment for the Nice festival where so many people of the nations come together.[21]

Above all, the Franco-Prussian War of 1870–71 had also exacerbated existing but dormant passions. As the French campaign went badly wrong there were repercussions even in the far southeastern border region. The confusion of loyalties and the simmering issues of nationality felt among some of the local inhabitants are well-illustrated by Winter. Daniel copied out part of a letter from Winter to give Thomas a flavour of local feeling while he was away in China:

There is surely no population in France more unsteady and inconsequent in its political opinions than that of Mentone and the environs. A fortnight ago the *Mentonais* were the most zealous Bonapartists (not only Imperialists). Today they are the most ardent Republicans. The bust of Napoleon III has been thrown down from its column in the *Place* – the municipal *Bureaux d' Octroi* [tax offices] have been burnt because their walls bore the imperial eagle. A stout young wife called '*la Turca*' marched with the red Republican banner at the head of a troop of women of the same mind to the mansion of a priest, and obliged him to cry with them, '*Vive la Republique*'. Another troop of people forced the Mayor to show them the list of inhabitants that received money from the Imperial Government for secret services. It is said that this list showed a number of 80, everyone of whom got frs1.50 per day. This would form the respectable sum of frs43,000 *per annum*. This seems incredible, but I learnt it from several men that pretended to be well informed. The *Commissaire de Police* has been gravely wounded in a quarrel he had with some *Mentonais*.

The people at Nizza is much more consequent than that of Mentone; its greatest wish is already long ago to return to Italy. The excitement is also great there. The *prefet* of Nizza and that of Marseilles fled by sea, in a little boat from Monaco to Italy. They debarked by Latte. At Ventimiglia 500 *bersaglieri* have arrived, and other troops are expected.[22]

For Winter this bloody war between France and Prussia, which led to Prussia's founding of the German Empire, was something more than a cause of local instability. Winter himself was Prussian and the proximity of the French border was a reason for some discomfort. Daniel Hanbury was concerned enough to inform Thomas on 19 August 1870 that: 'I have recommended to Winter not even to go into Mentone while people are so much excited about German spies.'[23]

The personal threat to Winter was not long-lasting, but it does emphasise the foreignness of this Prussian head gardener and, by association, of the garden and Thomas, to the locale and its inhabitants. In December 1868, as Winter began his job, Thomas had written: 'I generally speak French with Winter; he tries to make the men understand, but has not acquired much of their patois yet, I fear.'[24] The Englishman Thomas Hanbury, in his garden in Italy, was forced to speak French to his German head gardener, Ludwig Winter, in order that Winter might instruct, in the local patois, his Italian gardeners, who spoke no Italian. Part of Winter's success at La Mortola was not simply horticultural, but lay in overcoming all the cultural and social handicaps that faced him in communicating with both his staff and his employer. In achieving this Winter did much to bring the *Mortolati* and the Hanburys closer together.

Winter's letters were to prove informative and entertaining to both Thomas and Daniel, but they were also very important in helping Thomas to understand both his head gardener, and the others who lived and worked at La Mortola. Winter's literary style was often amusement enough in itself. Daniel remarks on one letter: 'from its quaintness we had a hearty laugh'; but he praises another for being 'well-told'. Here, for instance, Winter tells of a terrible storm that struck at La Mortola:

...clouds descended like gigantick torrents from the mountains, spreading thick darkness everywhere, momentaneously lighted up by sudden lightening followed of thunder strokes as tremendous I never heard before.

The walls of exposed houses literally trembled from the windshocks; – women fraid – children wept – and the bell of the Chiodi church rang supplicant tunes to heaven.[25]

Winter had a particular talent for relating the peculiarities of traditional village life in letters that often focus on the idiosyncrasies of the Church. Winter had experienced some difficulty in arranging a religious ceremony for his marriage, due, no doubt, to his Protestant heritage, which may have had a bearing on his subject matter. Nonetheless the letters provide a fascinating document of life in La Mortola and of the ambivalent way in which the Church was perceived. The superstitious belief in the magical power of priesthood was juxtaposed with a very pragmatic assessment of the strengths and weaknesses of the servants of the Church. The particular qualities of priests were judged on all manner of criteria. One new incumbent at La Mortola achieved immediate and unanimous approval from his congregation because of his ability to deliver a mass in a blistering 27 minutes, as opposed to his predecessors' rather more sedate time of three quarters of an hour.

In a letter to Daniel dated 22 July 1872 Winter describes a method of local pest control applied to a beetle with a taste for flowers on citrus trees:

> There is a monk at Ventimiglia who enjoys the renown to be able to destroy thoroughly all kinds of caterpillars and also this injurious beetle by benediction of the trees and the malediction of these animals. Last year some proprietors at Mortola and Grimaldi called in their utter despair this powerful man, the Padre Germanio, in their grounds where he pronounced his famous *Analema*, assuring the anxious neighbours of the infected properties, that he could expel the beetles into a desert field where they could not injure other human planting. This Hocus-pocus was rewarded by a liberal present of money and a splendid dinner. The best effect was expected for this year but the beetles seem to be quite insensible for these insults of their chivalrous race and make now their appearance in far greater number as any time before. In your Brother's property, the lemon flowers are not much attacked by insects as they find other flowers to which they give preference.[26]

Pest control was something of an issue for the people of La Mortola and the pests appeared in many different guises. Winter wrote to Thomas:

Last year I reported you about a '*Ciaraviglio*' (lynch demonstration as you might call it) punishing an old couple for its being seduced on one side by Amor, on the other by God Mammon to take Hymen's ties – which union I may observe aside had but a duration of a few weeks as the possessing old wife would not sell her properties to satisfy the expensive caprices of the old, lire-loving lavish Penetto – now if I was in a humourous disposition I should sketch with many comical details a similar demonstration that took place 3 days ago, the object of which was the '*reverendissimo*' Priest of the village, who – by some very indecent expressions of amorous passions towards some women at Mortola excited a general storm of indignation. The tumultary elements of this demonstration were almost the same as last year, but the introduction of a new instrument – an old *organetto* constructed perhaps at the end of the last century and having possibly performed already a voyage around the globe – was an addition much applauded by the old *Mortolati* who are much pleased with the progress of their youth – The *Ciaraviglio* was lasting till midnight. The amorous priest will leave la Mortola in a few days.[27]

While the end of 1871 had seen a growing understanding between the Hanbury brothers and Ludwig Winter, as to the future direction of the garden at La Mortola and its harmonious management, the year of 1875 marked a very different turn of fortune for the personal relationships of Thomas and the garden. Thomas's diary entry for 6 March 1875 includes the line: 'Daniel taken unwell went to bed early in the evening.' On 9 March Daniel Hanbury retired to his bed with a feverish chill. It soon became clear that this was more than a passing malady. Daniel had contracted typhoid fever. By 22 March Thomas was describing his brother's condition as 'precarious'. On 24 March Thomas wrote to Joseph Hooker:

> I sent you a telegram this afternoon to warn you how near his end my poor brother appeared to be. He passed away without struggle this evening at 7 o' clock.
>
> My dear parents altho' feeling their loss most acutely are wonderfully sustained.
>
> Dan gave me on the 18th, minute instructions regarding his funeral in case his illness should terminate fatally. He wished none but his parents + brothers + sisters to be present.[28]

The death of Daniel, in his 50th year, was the cause of a deep sadness in Thomas. Their mother, Rachel, is thought never to have overcome the loss of her eldest son. She died less than a year later. The profound nature of Thomas's relationship with his brother has been described in the previous chapter. His influence on the garden that was to be Thomas's footprint on the Riviera was no less significant. If Winter can be characterized as a landscaper and motivator, then Daniel was the primary source of the garden's botanic wealth. Daniel's network of friends and colleagues, nurtured over 25 years of scholarship, had provided Thomas's garden with access to plants and seeds from across the world. Daniel's own expertise and horticultural ambition had guided and encouraged Thomas's vision of La Mortola.

On 21 June 1875 Ludwig Winter left La Mortola to set up a plant nursery in Bordighera. His independent spirit had always yearned for such an enterprise and with the generous backing of Thomas it was made possible. Thomas continued to support Winter's business ventures for the rest of his life. The benefits of working for Thomas may not have been apparent in immediate income, but his friendship and loyalty made for endless recompense. This agreement of 1877 for the expansion of Winter's nursery seems typical of Thomas, extending a helping hand but not an extravagant freeload. Business-like but warm, he was a charitable capitalist:

> If I bought these three pieces[of land] it would be on condition that you rented them of me for five years at such a price as would give 5% interest for my outlay clear of all expenses and taxes.
>
> I should give you the right to buy the property at the end of five years at the sum it cost me, but on the other hand I should take away as my own profit in the transaction ten of the best palm trees.[29]

Thomas continued to lend Winter money regularly: 60,000 lire in 1895, 8,000 lire in 1897, 40,000 lire in 1905. He also recommended Winter both as a nurseryman and as a landscaper, even putting him forward as a candidate to lay out the municipal and botanic gardens in Pretoria, South Africa.

As an influential horticultural precedent, all three men looked to the garden of Gustave Thuret in Antibes. Thuret was a renowned botanist and had come to Antibes, with his colleague Dr Bornet, in 1857. There he had set about establishing an experimental garden for the acclimatization of new plant species. Daniel's botanical connections had brought him into contact and friendship with Thuret, and, from the very earliest days of the garden at La Mortola, Thuret's help and advice had proved most useful. Bountiful donations of plants and seeds were made by Thuret to the Hanburys. Villa Thuret was the standard by which the Hanburys judged and planned their own garden. As Thomas wrote to Thistleton-Dyer: 'I fear my poor garden was sadly effaced (as it always is) by the visit you paid I believe directly after to the rich collection at Antibes.'[30] Winter made his opinion clear to Thomas in a letter of 18 January 1875: 'Mr Thuret appears to be a botanical aristocrat and his garden a *refugium botanicum* for his botanical friends.'[31]

Thuret died in 1875. By July that year Thomas was looking to find a buyer for Villa Thuret, in order that the garden should not be lost. Thus, by the close of the year Thomas had lost his inspirational brother, his head gardener and his closest horticultural ally in the region. Thomas was now truly on his own at the helm of the gardens at La Mortola; he had also become the leading horticultural figure on the Riviera.

# Chapter Eight
# The pitiful want of water

Water will always dominate a garden, whether by its presence or by its absence. Water insinuates itself into every aspect of a garden, its plants, its soil, its topography and the artifice of its landscape. It matters not that the garden may be in a bog or a desert. The equable dampness of the British Isles is probably the single most important factor in accounting for their facility in spawning gardeners. The Moors, those incubators of European horticulture, made water not just the blood of their gardens but also the bones, as the Alhambra demonstrates so beautifully. A Moorish garden is an expression of power, primarily because it presupposes an abundant possession not of land but of water. The garden at La Mortola is no Alhambra, but water has moulded the garden nonetheless, and helped to fashion its design and planting.

The garden lies tucked in a limestone cleft that insulates the land from the ravages of winds from the north and northwest. It is a cradle carved out of the hillside over thousands of years of water erosion, which has produced La Mortola's steep ravine-like valley. When viewed from the hilltop village of Ciotti, which towers hundreds of feet above the palazzo and the garden, the extent of the protection afforded by this valley is striking. It is as if the garden has been folded into a fissure in the rock. The effects of water on limestone may have worn away a cosy niche for the palazzo, but the soil it has created is heavy, clay-like and not suited to many plants, which prefer a more acidic medium. It is a burnt-cream colour and, once dry, it cracks like subsiding plaster. In the summer the soil sets hard, clamping plants in its rocky grip, while rain or irrigation runs slickly off its surface. Any moisture absorbed drains quickly from the sloping ground.

When Thomas Hanbury first arrived, in 1867, it was March, early in the year, and the benefits of the spring and winter rains still lingered at La Mortola. However, the south-facing site was to pose some challenges to the Hanburys in the summer. Thomas was not unaware of these challenges and, as has been mentioned earlier (in Chapter 7), his initial instructions for the garden made much of the preparation of water tanks and the securing of water supplies. As Alwin Berger describes the garden in *Hortus Mortolensis*:

> ...generally speaking, the rainfall is irregular, and three months may pass with little or no rain, and this may happen not only during the summer but also in winter. The drought is often such that even large fleshy *Opuntias* become shrivelled and withered. No garden could exist under these conditions without an artificial water supply, and this is here provided by large tanks.[1]

The dryness of the site had most definite implications for the selection of garden plants. On 10 May 1868 Daniel, the plant savant, wrote to his botanist friend Spruce:

> I have been endeavouring to find what to recommend for my brother Thomas's grounds near Mentone, but it is not easy to note many shrubs with all the required qualifications. I want things that will grow easily, are not likely to be torn to atoms by the wind, nor

scorched to death by the sun, nor dried up by lack of rain for 3 or 4 months. Australian trees and shrubs are said to withstand drought in a wonderful manner and to grow withal at a fine pace. My brother has put in several *Eucalyptus – et nous verrons.*[2]

Thomas used different species of eucalyptus enthusiastically in the first 10 years at La Mortola. In fact, he planted 21 species of eucalyptus before the end of 1867. They grew with gusto, and quickly augmented the woody framework of olive and cypress that knitted the garden together. By 1880 there were more than 50 different species of eucalyptus at La Mortola and so vigorously had they grown that Thomas was forced to cut many of them down. The eucalyptus at La Mortola today stand in the belt of Australian trees and shrubs below the palazzo, and through the woodland on the western edge of the garden. *Eucalyptus globulus* is the dominant species. It makes a massive tree, its thick trunks ornamented by silvery bark streaked with greens, pinks, blues and browns. *E. globulus* is most adept at using any available moisture to its very fullest potential. The tough grey-blue leaves, heavily fragranced with pungent oils, help to lock that moisture within the tree. The result is furious growth as Berger recorded:

The largest specimen of *E. globulus*, on the main path leading down to the house, was planted in the spring of 1869; it was then 90cm high... On March 19th, 1873, it was found to have 75cm circumference at 1m above the soil; next year it was measured on March 6th, the stem was then 92cm in circumference and 14.65m high.[3]

The value of *E. globulus* to Thomas is clear, but the links between this tree and water were more significant still in 19th-century Italy and its struggle into modernity. Malaria was responsible for the deaths of 15,000 Italians every year. In the summer months parts of the countryside became uninhabitable, particularly in some regions of the south, where the disease could account for 20–30 per cent of deaths. Great chunks of land were affected. These areas were, of course, those suited to the mosquito, being warm and wet, but often also fertile land of great agricultural potential. The human and economic cost of malaria to Italy was huge. It was a measure of the national disruption wreaked by this disease that the capital city, Rome, was perceived to be so riddled with malaria as to be avoided or evacuated by all persons of good sense during the summer. Some 56 kilometres from Rome lay the Pontine Marshes, in whose swampy atmosphere malaria flourished. The actual cause of malaria and its transmission by mosquitoes was then still undiscovered, but the powerful oils of the eucalyptus were believed to keep the deadly miasma at bay. Thomas wrote to a friend, Cuthbertson, in Australia:

> I am very much interested in all you write about Australia, there is quite a fever to get the Eucalyptus, the gum tree you so much despise, it is thought extremely valuble for its febrifugal properties and notices of its wonderful properties are constantly appearing in the papers. You will recollect we have many at La Mortola.[4]

The link between the illness and marshes had been made, but the accepted understanding was that malaria was about bad air, literally *mal aria*. One of Ludwig Winter's earliest money-making schemes was a nursery solely for the production of eucalyptus. Thomas declined to invest in the project. In contrast, so confident in the febrifugal powers of the eucalyptus were the Trappist monks of the Basilica of Tre Fontane that in the 1870's they began to plant hundreds of *E. globulus* in the Pontine Marshes. A number of the monks succumbed to the disease during the execution of this scheme, but nonetheless after many years there occurred a noticeable depreciation in the number of cases of malaria. The success of *E. globulus* in combating malaria depended absolutely on the trees' ability to use the available water. The eucalyptus formed a living drainage system that removed the mosquitoes' breeding habitat. By 1935 Mussolini's regime had turned the area of the Pontine Marshes into the jewel in his land reclamation crown, populating it with small farms.

Dr Bennet is most insistent that in Menton (as it had been renamed) cases of malaria were mostly restricted to the few sufferers who had contracted the disease elsewhere in the Mediterranean. Most foreign visitors returned north well before the violent heat of the summer in any case. Interestingly, Bennet does comment on the rise of what he refers to as 'intermittent fever':

> Until within the last few years intermittent fever was all but unknown, but for several summers there have been many cases. This is a very singular fact, difficult to account for on the marsh theory, as there are no marshes or plains in the district. Some of the cases have occurred in mountain villages such as Grimaldi, perched on the rock side 700 feet high.

Bennet is rather at a loss to explain how these fevers might be caused without 'the marsh miasmatas' that he associates with the natural occurrence of this disease. This is made all the more peculiar by the recent surge in incidence:

> It has been suggested that the great increase of tanks of stagnant water for irrigation, owing to the increased prosperity of the country during the last few years, may be the cause of this recent manifestation of ague in the summer heats.[5]

This unfortunate link between the advance of prosperity and water-assisted disease had a national resonance. The evidence of increased occurrence of malaria in Italy towards the end of the 19th century has been linked in some areas to the huge increase in the number of drainage ditches, required to flank its new railway lines. In 1870 Italy had a railway network comprising 6,400 kilometres of track. By 1890 this figure had more than doubled, to 13,600 kilometres.[6] As the railway expanded so did the muddy channels alongside the tracks, which became home to millions of mosquito larvae.

Malarial or not, mosquitoes around Menton were considered enough of a plague to warrant their own chapter in the Reverend Casey's *Riviera Nature Notes* (1903) and to merit comment from Thomas as to their increase, the result of ever-swelling ranks of hotels and villas with their cesspools. The water tanks for the garden, therefore, were not without their disadvantages. Thomas insisted on keeping carp to eat any mosquito larvae in his irrigation tanks and was a great believer in the mosquito net, both stemming from his days in China.

As an understanding of the role of mosquitoes in the spread of malaria developed, towards the end of the 19th century, so the control of the mosquito population became of greater importance. Thomas noted in his diary on 21 October 1898: 'Row with Giacomo + Angelina about mosquitoes in cess pool.' The problem of mosquitoes was viewed as a threat to local livelihoods serious enough, to warrant a meeting on the subject, convened by the Mayor of Menton on 28 April 1899.

Incidences of typhoid and cholera were not uncommon in Italy and France, and the contamination of drinking water was a significant element in the transmission of both diseases. In 1875 Dr Bennet was able to write confidently: 'Asiatic cholera has never appeared at Mentone, a rather singular fact, as it exercised considerable ravages on most other parts of the Riviera.'[7] Menton may have avoided cholera at that point, but complacency offered no immunity to disease. The epidemic of Asiatic cholera that had begun in India in 1879 reached the Mediterranean in 1883. On 25 June in the latter year Thomas wrote in his diary: 'Heard that cholera had broken out in Toulon.' Four days later he received a visit from the mayors of Ventimiglia and San Remo, and the Prefect of Porto Maurizio, who all wanted to produce a coherent quarantine policy. A temporary railway station was set up at Latte and the Menton border post at the Ponte San Luigi was closed. On 3 July 1884 Thomas recorded in his diary that 'All persons were stopped and turned back'. Thomas himself left with his family for Britain, via Switzerland. Their train was fumigated heavily twice before they crossed the border out of Italy. In July 1884 a worried Professor Fluckiger wrote to Thomas in relation to the deadly outbreak of cholera: 'We are extremely anxious to learn positively that you have – as we hope you did – in due time left the south for the safe regions of the United Kingdom.' Sadly, not everyone could escape to healthier climes: between 1884 and 1886 cholera killed more than 50,000 Italians.

Typhoid had already claimed Daniel, Thomas's beloved brother and Fluckiger's sometime co-author, at Clapham in 1875 (see Chapter 6). Fourteen years earlier the same disease, fostered in the drains of Buckingham Palace, had taken Prince Albert from the nation and his Queen. Now, on 18 October 1881, Thomas wrote to Thistleton-Dyer about the family's summer holiday at Macugnaga by Monte Rosa, 'where my wife and eldest son unfortunately got typhoid fever from which they are now slowly recovering, I nursed them for nearly seven weeks'. Cecil had succumbed first and, indicating how common malaria was, the boy was first diagnosed as having that disease. Thomas was a conscientious, knowledgeable and caring nurse, but the strain and anxiety of having both his wife and their son suffering from typhoid simultaneously must have been immense. Memories of his brother's death can never have been far from his thoughts.

In 1887 27,000 Italians died from typhoid. Public sanitation was rudimentary. Domestic and human waste was often dealt with in the most basic and peremptory way. The traditional method of dealing with sewage in villages such as La Mortola was to use it as manure in the more distant olive and citrus groves. As was so often the case in the garden at La Mortola, Thomas followed the example of Gustave Thuret: 'Earth closet earth for manuring the Palm trees for which M. Thuret says it is valuable.'[8]

The provision of drinking fountains by Thomas at La Mortola, Grimaldi, Latte and Ventimiglia was, therefore, not simply a thoughtful gesture to parched travellers. These fountains represented secure and hygienic sources of drinking water for the local population and, as such, would have been of great benefit to them. Tap water was almost entirely unknown to the poor inhabitants of these communities and for many people the fountains made the daily grind of fetching water considerably less arduous. For example, La Fontana del Olivio, built by Thomas outside the garden gates at La Mortola in 1877, took a mile off the round trip to the spring that the villagers had previously had to make.

The broader commitment to public health that Thomas had demonstrated in Shanghai was shown again in Italy. Thomas gave extremely generously to the hospital at Ventimiglia throughout his life in Italy, providing money, medicine and equipment. In 1893 he was elected President of the Ventimiglia Hospital and after his death the hospital received another 50,000 lire.

As I witnessed for myself last summer, lack of water is simply a fact of life at La Mortola. Winter referred to 'the greatest defect of Mortola – the pitiful want of water'.[9] Yet this 'defect' is one of the garden's tremendous characteristics. Plants that define the garden are themselves defined by the conditions within that garden. Thomas understood his garden's demands and his golden rule for the garden was 'Never go against Nature'. In some ways this is a strange choice for any gardener, as a garden, by definition, is against nature and for artifice. For Thomas this meant that, for a dry garden, plants used to an arid environment were required. Succulent plants, with their ability to store water, were ideal and they were to become Thomas's favourites.

The cactus and the aloe are, perhaps, the most familiar and celebrated of this group of plants, but my own favourite, a plant that has become, not just an emblem of La Mortola, but a familiar sight throughout the Riviera, is the agave. By the end of 1871 there were 40 different species and subspecies of agave in the garden. For grace under the fire of drought, no plant in the garden at La Mortola is the equal to the agave. A native of Mexico, Central America, the West Indies and the arid western United States, the agave fascinates both the eye and the imagination, in a manner that implies significance beyond the plant world. No one has felt this significance more than the Aztecs did. They deified the agave in the form of the goddess Mayahuel, in tribute to the beneficent nature of a plant that provided food, clothing, drinks both refreshing and alcoholic, shelter, and much more. Such was the perception of Mayahuel's fecund generosity that she was characterized by an endowment of 400 nipples, offering nourishment to a nation. Today the agave still provides Mexico and the world with millions of litres of tequila, miles of sisal and a host of other products, stretching even to a Californian version of the didgeridoo. As a thing of beauty, also, the agave has proved itself most constant.

For the vast majority of the agave's 250 species the basic form is simple: a near stemless rosette of succulent, sword-shaped leaves. The rosette of the largest species can stand two metres high, with a spread of more than 4m, the smallest being as low as 10–15 cm by 15–20 cm wide. Only once in the life of most agaves do they flower, producing from the centre of a whorl of leaves a single flowering stem that can achieve heights of 12 metres. The longevity of some of these monocarpic species gained the genus its common name of the 'century plant'.

It was a popular misconception that the agave lived for 100 years before deigning to flower. The truth is slightly less impressive, as different species require differing periods of maturation. The larger the species, the longer it takes. The rough average across the species, however, has been given as eight to 20 years. In 1999, *A. salmiana* flowered in the Abbey Gardens, Tresco, when it was more than 50 years old. The clump forming *A. celsii*, however, produces a flowering stem from a rosette that is less than 10 years old.

The agave could be compared to a chlorophyll-powered pump, akin to a child's water rocket. Its rigid succulent leaves, the power transformers, are held fast by the energy stored in anticipation of the agave's dramatic and fatal flowering. As the stem is produced and the flowers open, the pump deflates. The inflorescence heads for the heavens, and the exhausted leaves wilt and wither in its wake. The flowering stems are to be found in two main forms: spicate, a single, unbranched spike of flowers, and paniculate, a candelabra-like arrangement of branched flowerheads.

The agave can be unforgiving to the touch. Many species are armed with an array of barbs and teeth on the leaf margins, and are tipped with a terminal spine. The smooth leaf surface feels cold and hard, like the flank of a dead shark. Often the patterns of the formidable thorns are delicately imprinted on the leaves as they unfurl from the rosette's centre. This ghostly trace of the leaf's protracted birth serves as an elegant reminder of the agave's stately life cycle. Since the agave is a monocarpic plant, its single flowering qualifies it as a time-lapse annual: a Methuselah for the ephemeral generations. Each leaf, having spent two to three years in bud, may live for up to 15 years.

The agave has been in cultivation in Europe since the 1570s, but its use in its native habitat stretches back thousands of years. From about 7000 BC the agave was a staple ingredient in the diet of native Mexican and other American peoples, providing, at times, 25–50 per cent of all food ingested. As an intoxicant the agave has been imbibed in the form of *pulque* since AD 1000. Pulque played an important role in the Aztecs' culture, fuelling many of their brutal religious ceremonies. With the Spanish conquest came distillation and the production of tequila. The fibrous elements of the leaves provide sisal, while the cuticle of some species can be used to wrap food, much like an organic cling film. The leaves have offered human beings the wherewithal to manufacture such articles as rope, roof tiles, needles, soap and even musical instruments.

The agave is not, perhaps, the most suitable option for a child-centred garden, but then neither is the thorny rose. The fearsome defensive display of the agave belies its inherent magnanimity. There is something of the Old Testament that possesses the agave: terrible as an army with banners, yet still the source of life and succour in the wilderness. The agave takes its name from the Greek for 'illustrious' or 'noble'; it brings a sense of majesty as well as ornament to a garden. To use the word 'architectural' in reference to a plant these days is to pay court to cliché, so ubiquitous is its application. Yet if one can accept, at least, that a plant's aesthetic worth can be described in terms related to architecture, then the agave is nothing less than a temple.[10]

The issue of water for the garden was to embroil Thomas in disputes that ranged beyond plant choices and horticulture. For everybody at La Mortola the same source that Thomas used to water his plants provided them with the water for all their needs: all their drinking, cooking and washing water came from the local springs and streams. Water was also physical power, driving the heavy millstones in the olive mills. For the *Mortolati* water provided the means by which they could transform their hard and bitter black olives into the 'green gold' of olive oil. The demands on the water supply and its finite nature made water a sensitive political issue.

In February 1870 Daniel wrote to Thomas:

> Lorenzi writes to me that the people of Ciotti have commenced legal proceedings against the proprietors of the oil mills at Mortola in order to deprive the latter of certain rights to water – and he has asked my sanction to employ Cabagni to represent thee in the case.[11]

In October Daniel wrote again about:

> the dispute arisen between the people of Ciotti and those of Mortola relative to the water, to which after the feast of St Michael, the latter village declares itself entitled. It seems that Cabagni was to be appealed to and then the *Juge de Paix* – and

after that it might be necessary to get the assistance of some 'carabineers' to enforce a surrender of the coveted water.[12]

The conflict between the two villages and the legal actions it gave rise to were to continue for another three years. Thomas desperately attempted to remain removed from this bitter internecine row, hoping that doing so might allow him to play the role of diplomatic intermediary.

Thomas had not acquired, by any measure, all the land around the palazzo and garden in 1867. Odd strips and parcels of land remained in the possession of disparate individuals, and the complicated history of ownership and boundaries often made the sale of land torturous. Thomas's wealth and his desire to consolidate his property into a cohesive unit encouraged unrealistic evaluations of the land by vendors. A businessman and real estate dealer of Thomas's enormous skill was not going to be forced into paying an inflated price through impatience. As a result he found himself drawn further into local politics than he might have wished. This letter, from Thomas to another landowner, Cabagni, is a testament to Thomas's exasperation with the divisive and complex nature of such disputes:

I am sorry that you have thought it necessary to bring a lawsuit to try to force me to pay a portion of the expenses incurred by yourself and others of the Mortola people in the action against those of Ciotti, for I said distinctly a year since that I would not join in the action.

As I am starting tomorrow for England I have requested Signr Laura to defend me against your action, but before leaving I wish to inform you that, regretting very much the ill-feeling that this miserable affair causes between the population of the two villages of Mortola Superiore [Ciotti] & Inferiore (people who should live in neighbourly friendship), I have proposed a compromise between the litigants as follows.

1st The water of the source to belong to Mortola Inferiore from December to June and to Mortola Superiore the remaining six months of the year.

2nd The people of Mortola Superiore to pay the people of Mortola Inferiore 1,000 L.- compensation for the use of water for the past four years. Each side to pay its own law expenses.

3rd On a final settlement being made I will pay to those of Mortola Inferiore & to yourself the sum of Lire 300 and give up my share of Lire 1000 which share I presume is estimated at about Lire 350.

4th The pending return against me at Ventimiglia to be abandoned and no further attempts to be made to force me to become a party to the process or to charge me expenses in this affair which I have always refused to enter on.

I am happy to say that people both of Mort.Sup + Mort.Inf after due consideration are quite content to settle the whole affair on the above terms. I have therefore the more pleasure of bringing the arrangement to your notice feeling sure that you will also agree to end this litigation which for nearly four years has caused so much loss of time, trouble and ill-feeling in this neighbourhood.[13]

If water was still the source of mechanical power for the production of olive oil, the eternal life blood of Liguria, then water was to be the key to a power altogether as revolutionary for Italy as the olive was traditional. Hydroelectricity, from the mountains of the north, was to be known as Italy's 'white coal': it became a major factor in making Italy's industrial goods competitive in the European and world markets. In the 1890s this inexhaustible supply of energy boosted investment and was the focus of national pride. Milan became only the second city in the world to be illuminated by the light of electric street lamps. In 1896 an English company, Woodhouse & Baillie, began to supply hydro-electric power to Ventimiglia. The first generating turbine was set up and housed in an old olive mill. The streets of Ventimiglia were lit in 1897 and trams were running by 1898. The following year Thomas became involved in the further development of the tram scheme, con-ducting talks with the *Sindaco* (mayor), Mr Woodhouse, Mr Baillie, F. Notari and his own nephew, Arthur Hanbury. In 1901 Thomas gave financial and moral support to the setting up of the Alassio Electric Supply Company, the managing directors of which were Arthur Hanbury and his son Daniel. By the end of 1901 Thomas had invested more than £6,000 in his son's company.

Thomas was not a man to step away from a sound profit-making ven-ture. Although he had taken a step back from the management of his property in China, his love of business had never left him. As the pop-ularity of the Riviera grew and grew, so Thomas's talents as a shrewd investor helped him to develop his property portfolio. He owned a size-able amount of land in Ventimiglia, but his purchases in Alassio demon-strate that his old Shanghai real estate skills were still functioning effectively. As the railway brought more British tourists further east along the Riviera coast, Thomas saw the potential for developing the seaside village of Alassio into a tasteful resort. Between 1879 and 1888 he purchased nearly 85 square kilometres of land in and around Alassio, on which he built villas and even a hotel. By 1901 the British commu-nity that had adopted Alassio formed a large, willing and wealthy pool of clients for the new Hanbury purveyors of hydroelectricity.

Not all that Thomas touched turned to gold, however, even when he was dealing in 'white coal'. Thomas had led a business syndicate buying property in the Valle d'Aosta in the 1880s. They had acquired three copper mines and a concession for supplying water for the production of hydroelectric power. The venture was not a success and, after Thomas managed to sell the mines in June 1897, he wrote in his diary: 'Bade a final farewell to Pont St. Martin where I have lost so much money.' Nevertheless, such downturns in his business fortunes were unusual. He not only invested in the new phenomenon of large-scale electricity supply, he also involved himself, for example, in the improvement of the local roads.

While the desire to make money never dimmed in Thomas, the benefits of his wealth to others never slackened either. The Alassio Electric Supply Company became mains-connected on 28 June 1901. On 9 July the electric lights of the private subscribers in Alassio were lit for the first time at 8.12 pm. At 8.41 pm the public lighting in the streets was illuminated.[14] To Thomas this may well have appeared as yet another example of the heels of technological advance and capitalism being followed closely by public good.

Most of the developments in life on this stretch of Liguria were far in advance of what was happening in most areas of rural Italy. The improvements in the infrastructure along the coast came from the capital brought by foreigners' great affection for the Riviera; and no one was more affectionate than the British. Led by ill health, fashion or social aspirations, the wintering British helped to transform part of Italy. None of them did more than Thomas. There can be few symbols of a changing Liguria more potent than that of a hydroelectric turbine running in a now redundant olive mill. For La Mortola, Liguria and Italy, water and its use were the future.

# Chapter Nine
# The taint of opium and fruit of Shanghai

'The vessel we are going to China in from this place is a paddle-steamer, called the 'Malta'. She is about the same size as the 'Bombay', but a much cleaner and nicer boat, and we have much more room, in consequence of the Calcutta passengers having left us. There is a disagreeable smell of opium, in consequence of there being a great deal in the hold which is going to China.'[1]

Thomas had boarded the *Malta* at Galle, in what was then Ceylon (now Sri Lanka), on his first journey to Shanghai in 1853. The cargo of opium was to dominate the voyage. The heavily laden ship was sluggish and slow. The cheap cabins occupied by Thomas and his colleagues were made less comfortable by the huge weight of opium in the hold. Their portholes were now so close to the water that they were forbidden to open them, however stifling the tropical heat might become. The opium exuded a thick aroma that lingered in the airless quarters below decks. Passengers complained of feeling strangely soporific, and prone to headaches and nausea. The pall of opium clung to the ship all the way to China. Its taint was pervasive.

The central role played by the opium trade in the opening up of China to western traders has been discussed previously (in Chapter 2). The Quaker abhorrence of immorality, which made Thomas so appalled at the excesses of Shanghai's debauchery and the violence among and against the Chinese, also led to his seeking to avoid any direct dealings in the traffic of opium. As with the market-led military intervention and political cynicism that characterized European and US policy in China, opium infiltrated, influenced and maintained all the trade for foreign companies, whatever moral high ground they chose to claim.

In 1854 Thomas replied to his father's request that their business should be unsullied by the opium trade. They were trading in bonds and currency:

> I notice thou dost not wish any of thy money used in the opium trade but the remittance sent viz. Compys Rupees are used almost solely for sending to India in payment for the drug by Parsees.[2]

The dependence on opium to provide the foreign traders with the silver to buy tea and silk was extremely high. Thomas was to find in early 1854 that, when the opium market faltered, all markets faltered:

> Thou wilt doubtless have read in the newspapers ere this reaches thee of the extraordinary discipline of the Insurgents at Nankin, and the strict prohibitions against the use of both opium and tobacco, this is even beginning to be felt here, and the deliveries of the drug for the past year have fallen off to a big degree, should this continue we shall require some medium to supply in its place. Imports of Manchester goods there is at present scarcely any demand for, and they cannot be moved off except at a con-

siderable reduction on cost price, this of course has caused an almost total cessation of imports from England, and large quantities of silver have been needed for the purchase of Tea and Silk...[3]

Opium was very much part of Shanghai life. As Thomas was able to relate to a meeting on 19 January 1875 of the Anglo-Oriental Society for the Suppression of the Opium Trade (AOSSOT), of which he was one of the founding members, the addictive habit of opium-smoking was common in Shanghai and, in some ways, accepted:

I myself have known opium-smokers of 20 years standing who retained all their mental faculties, although their physical powers had been rendered extremely weak. Some of the cleverest men of business in Shanghai are inveterate smokers of opium, and so strong a hold has the habit got of them, that they are incapable of commencing the business of the day until they have smoked one or more pipes.[4]

The trade and use of opium was not limited to China. Members of the Hanbury family themselves were no strangers to dealing in opium, but did so strictly in relation to its capacity as a medicine, rather than as a recreational drug. The London opium market was long-established, and a pharmacy of the size of Allen & Hanbury would have made regular and sizeable purchases of the opium. Opium was used in the production of a large selection of medicines around the world. For example, during the devastating cholera and dysentery epidemic that raged around Shanghai in September 1862 opium-based medicines, such as laudanum, were the standard curatives. During periods of illness Thomas and Daniel both administered themselves with opiates if they saw fit.

Opiates were readily available in Britain, in a bewildering number of guises. A letter from a fellow botanist, Dr Richard Spruce, to Daniel Hanbury offers a startling example of opiate confectionery:

At our village shop 'Aniseed Drops' are sold to children & I am pretty sure they have opium in them. There is still too little responsibility in the purchase of powerful drugs.[5]

It was easy to grow accustomed to the ubiquity of opium and in the eyes of many of Thomas's contemporaries the trade in opium was not iniquitous or, at least, no more so than the trade in alcohol. Indeed, many wondered why such a fuss was made of opium in China, when the abuse of alcohol was such an appalling problem in Britain.

At that meeting of the AOSSOT in January 1875 Thomas was able to assert with some confidence that he had never imported a single chest of opium into China. It is recorded that this declaration was met with a resounding chorus of 'Hear, hear!' I have no doubt that this statement is absolutely accurate. There could not have been many other traders in those early days of a British presence in Shanghai who could make a similar assertion. The opium trade, however, spread itself thinly and eventually seeped into the lives of most people in Shanghai. The assumption of many was that any money from China was inevitably soiled with opium. Even today most people smirkingly and instinctively relate wealth derived from 19th-century China with opium.

When Thomas became an active and vociferous member of the AOSSOT there were some who would have sneered at his taking a stand against the trade. Thomas was not a popular figure with the more brutal pursuers of riches in China, those for whom the Chinese represented an inexhaustible but individually expendable mass of consumers and nothing more. Of the 13 million pounds of opium imported into China in the 1870s 'more than half of it entered through Shanghai'.[6] Thomas was seeking to end the monopoly of opium manufacture and supply that was the cornerstone of the city's wealth. Thomas had been the tax collector for the Municipal Council. He regularly contributed to the letters page of the *Times*, attacking the one-dimensional and rapacious policies adopted in China by the European powers. Given his life-long and very public support for more honest, conciliatory and amicable relations with the Chinese, there were many trading in China who would have relished an opportunity to silence him.

Property was the means by which Thomas had secured his fortune in Shanghai. He had become the city's largest private landowner, having nearly 1,500 houses on his rent roll. The houses were often to be found in the less well-heeled areas and were leased by Chinese rather than Europeans. This was the land that Thomas had acquired very cheaply during the various slumps in property prices that had occurred in the 1860's. Thomas was quite content to concentrate on this end of the market, remarking to Iveson in a letter dated 9 January 1874: 'I do not like the bother of European tenants.' Tenants varied from the wealthy to the poor, but they all tended to share Chinese nationality. After his return from Shanghai to La Mortola in 1871 Thomas had begun to relinquish all the running of his Shanghai property to the firm of Iveson & Company. By 1874 the old firm of Bower & Hanbury had ceased trading. In a letter dated 23 January 1874, one of the last he was to write to his employees at this firm, soon to be transformed into Iveson & Company, Thomas declared: 'I do not care to have the same class of tenants as before.'

It was through this property empire and its tenants that Thomas was to find himself under attack. The task of keeping his tenants respectable and his property free of opium dens and brothels was a Herculean one. Since the arrival of the western traders vice had thrived in Shanghai. The European community had made opium and prostitution hugely profitable trades in Shanghai, but the purveyors of these commodities, at street level, were mainly Chinese. The properties they sought to rent were away from respectable European residences and thus just the sort of areas that Thomas might own. At one time, as has been seen above, Thomas was perhaps less concerned about the manner by which his tenants earned their rent. This had changed, but Thomas was now thousands of miles away and unlikely to carry out any spot checks on the thoroughness of his property agents' work.

Any fraying of the moral fibre of Thomas's property portfolio seems to have gone undetected until as late as 1887. It was then that rumours reached Thomas that the part of Shanghai in which there was the highest concentration of his properties had become known as the 'Hanbury Quarter'. It was, allegedly, a locale associated with just the sort of depravity that Thomas hoped had been expunged from the hundreds of shops and houses that he owned. It was implied that the high rents charged forced tenants into immoral employment. Such accusations or gossip cast a rather dishonourable light on the livelihood and reputation of one who was both a Quaker and still a prominent supporter of the AOSSOT. Thomas wrote to Iveson & Company, demanding to know if there was any truth in the allegations. His agents denied strenuously that such an area even existed. Thomas wrote again on 9 March 1888, re-emphasizing his orders on the subject of brothels and opium dens:

I have written from time to time prohibiting your letting my houses for these purposes. Have my orders been carried out to the letter? If not I now desire you will no longer neglect to do so. If any remain let them have notice to quit.[7]

In reply, his agent, Walter C. Ward, wrote on 20 April 1888 that none of the properties was being used for such practices:

It is possible that through some misconception 'Hanbury Road' may have become converted into 'Hanbury Quarter' – a place which, as I have said, has no existence. The district is a poor one, as you know, the residents there being of the hard-working coolie class, and any idea that we exact high rents from tenants with a view to condoning their occupying their houses for immoral purposes is quite at variance with facts.[8]

J. Ambrose, another agent, wrote on the same day:

Without braggadacio on my part; I say there is no foreigner here knows Shanghai and all its ins and outs so well as I do, and if there was or had there been such a place I <u>must</u> have known it.

The only place I know of with 'Hanbury' attached to it is 'Hanbury Road' but <u>no-one</u> could for a moment think that the houses on this road were used for immoral purposes, as you well know, they are of the poorest class, and occupied by the labouring classes and small shopkeepers.[9]

The reassurance that Thomas must have felt on reading these letters was to evaporate two years later. In April 1890 he received some worrying correspondence from a friend, George Gillett. Gillett was in close contact with Alfred S. Dyer, who was in China in order to seek an interview with the Emperor, but also to expose and campaign against any corruption, moral, financial or political, that he might encounter. In May 1890 Dyer was to publish a virulent attack on the state of Shanghai, and the sordid and exploitative nature of many of its British residents, under the title 'A "Model" Infidel British Settlement'. Knowing that this piece was to be published, Gillett sought to bring some of Dyer's complaints to Thomas's attention. The name 'Hanbury' is not mentioned in Dyer's article, but Dyer had communicated privately to Gillett his view that there were elements of Thomas's Shanghai business inconsistent with his reputation for moral rectitude. In addition, earlier in 1890 Dyer had put forward a resolution at the annual meeting of the Shanghai Municipal Council that attempted to lessen the prevalence of brothels and opium dens. According to Gillett, Thomas's land agent, E. A. Probst, had greatly disappointed Mr. Dyer: 'Amongst those who voted in favour of opium dens and houses of ill fame, your agent figures for the largest number of votes given by any one voter.'[10]

The highly embarrassing association between Thomas and Probst, given Probst's public support for toleration of opium and prostitution was easily rectified: it could be convincingly explained that Probst was the voting agent for many other individuals as well as for Thomas, 26 in fact. Probst had simply cast his votes as a block. The agents were not at the forefront of the anti-opium campaign and men like Dyer were generally most unwelcome in Shanghai. In any case, Dyer's resolution had been defeated by a wide margin, with only 16 votes in favour and 160 against. The resolution had never stood a chance of success and seems to have been an exercise in publicity rather than a serious attempt at reform.

A more disturbing revelation came shortly afterwards. Gillett wrote:

the City Chamberlain Mr Scott, informed him that a lady resident of Shanghai for two years, whose husband lived there for 30, remarked that if the bad houses on Mr Hanbury's land were closed, the place would be quite transformed.[11]

Thomas's reputation as an honourable and honest man had been a large factor in his success in China. The *hong* he had created was called 'Kung Ping', meaning 'fair dealing'. He was now a man of considerable standing in Liguria. His house and garden had been visited by Queen Victoria, the Prince of Wales and many other members of European royal and noble families, and he had been decorated by the King of Italy. He was also still on the executive committee of the AOSSOT. Thomas lived by his reputation. This sort of insidious drawing-room gossip and venomous chatter must have been maddening. It was impossible for Thomas to defend himself against it or to combat it. Worse still, it might just be true.

Thomas wrote to Iveson & Company once again, asking for an explanation. On 6 June 1890 he requested that an inventory of all his Shanghai properties be made, with descriptions of what businesses were conducted in them. Then, on 20 August 1890, the following appeared in the *North China Daily News*:

> The *Chen Pao* tells its readers that 'the foreign "Kung Ping" is the owner of much house property in the Settlement. We hear its former partner Mr Hanbury, who has returned to England, has sent a telegram to China ordering that in future no opium shops are to be allowed on his premises, and that keepers of opium houses already established there are to receive one month's notice to quit. It is said that the reason for this order is that Mr Hanbury is one of the Committee of the British Anti-Opium Society.'

Not only did this English-language report of an article in a Chinese-language newspaper advertise Thomas's problems, it also carried the obvious implication that there were opium dens to be closed down. Perhaps the land agents had not been carrying out Thomas's orders with the efficiency that he would have expected.

The process of assessing all of Thomas's tenants was a laborious one and the final list was not sent until 14 November 1890. It has returns from 1,462 different houses. The agents had had more than five months to clean up the rent rolls. Thomas had instructed Ambrose at the Iveson office in Shanghai to carry out the detailed survey of his tenants. A letter from Ambrose that accompanied the final list shows the problems involved in compiling such an inventory, and the difficulties that Iveson & Company must have had in keeping Thomas's property 'clean' in a city like Shanghai. The letter runs to 11 pages of closely packed text. The summary of the returns from the 1,462 properties includes details of 41 rice dealers, seven Daoist priests, 12 barbers, 14 native doctors, four dealers in pearls , among other traders and providers of services to the Chinese residents. However, the list also includes 10 opium brokers and dealers, whose presence is not commented on by Thomas or Ambrose, as they were clearly legitimate traders for the medicine markets. The problems began, as Ambrose wrote to Thomas, with the large number of houses – 503, or more than one third of the total – that are described as 'private houses'. Ambrose complained that it was impossible:

> to ascertain from the occupants what their business or work their husbands are engaged in… it would have taken me six or nine months to worm out of them even partially correct replies…but with reference to those houses so returned you may rest perfectly assured that: <u>not one of them are opium shops or brothels.</u>
>
> The native staff has more or less trouble always in keeping your property free from brothels as intending clients knowing the

rules do not apply themselves, but send a respectable friend who takes the house for his 'number two or three wife' but when in possession the occupants shew their true means of living, and then there is trouble ejecting them.[12]

Unfortunately for Thomas and Ambrose, two properties are referred to as being occupied by 'Soochow Women', who on one such property 'occupy the principal number of houses'. These women were prostitutes, and their presence, as Ambrose observes, 'after your positive instructions to remove all such from your houses, you would no doubt like explained.' Ambrose then launched into a defence of this oversight, with what could be interpreted as a veiled attack on Thomas:

> On my arrival in Shanghai to take charge of your property amongst others, I found in it a very large number of Opium shops and brothels, to which there does not appear to have been any objection, and the first intimation I received that you did not desire your houses occupied as such, was in your letter of 21st March 1879, when in writing on the rebuilding of the eastern side of your Louzan Bridge property you said 'I do not wish the new houses let as opium dens if it can possibly be avoided', and the next intimation was I believe in your letter of 24th March 1887, when in writing on the rebuilding of m/c Block 73 Hongkew you said 'I forbid any of the new buildings being let as Opium dens or brothels', but your letter of 9th March 1888 contained the first direct order not to let any of your houses for opium dens or brothels, and to clear out any such that remained, so that up to the latter date I might have taken your instructions literally, and enforced the prohibition of such houses only in the blocks

specially mentioned. This I did not do, but upon every and all possible occasions, either when rebuilding, or when a tenant of such a house left, refused to allow the house to be occupied again for such purposes... I gradually weeded out the objectionable class of tenant, until now without loss to yourself, none remain except in the previously mentioned two properties.[13]

Thomas had certainly been, at one time, less particular concerning his tenants. Since 1874, however, he had expressed his wishes for this to change. In 1888 he had said unequivocally that his properties were to be emptied of prostitutes and opium dens. Most of the less wealthy tenants were on monthly leases. By 1889, at the very latest, this issue should surely have been completely resolved. Yet this had not been done. It is possible that Ambrose simply did not want Thomas to lose rent by leaving property empty. However, not to have cleared out the brothels and opium dens was to have disobeyed Thomas's orders.

Thomas would have been very well aware, of course, that the Settlement in Shanghai was its own world. Corruption and bribery, like whores and narcotics, were parts of the landscape. There were many people for sale in Shanghai, not just prostitutes. People saw things differently there. Looked at in a Shanghai light, the anti-opium lobby was displaying a hypocritical hysteria. China seemed awash with 'do gooding' bodies, such as the AOSSOT, which were dismissed by many in the International Settlement as groups of ignorant meddlers. The claim was that they failed to understand Shanghai and China, like the hordes of missionaries who had come to China only to squabble among themselves over what name to give God in Chinese. Few of the Chinese were impressed. Among the Quakers in western China, for instance, one station in Chonquing converted just 10 Chinese in seven years. This worked out at less than one convert per missionary. Most 'converts' accepted whatever food was on offer and then walked away: indeed, 'one of the would-be Quakers did so with some panache and set up an opium den down the street which he named Fu Yin Tang – Gospel Hall.'[14] In China opium was the religion of some of the masses, at least.

Many Europeans, including Ambrose, saw alcohol abuse in Britain as being far more destructive than opium abuse in China. Ambrose wrote to Thomas, in his epic letter of 14 November 1890:

> I consider that the trade in Opium is as legitimate a one as that in Wine or Beer, and a good deal less objectionable than the sale of spirits. Prior to my arrival here, I had superintendence of a number of working men, and I can honestly say I saw more vice in them, and more misery and want in their families caused entirely through the use of intoxicating liquors, than I have ever seen from the use of opium here, and from the many opportunities I have had of seeing the effects of both, consider myself perfectly qualified to give an opinion.

It is easy to see how, in the unique environment of Shanghai, thousands of miles away from England and from La Mortola, the absolute necessity of following Thomas's instructions may have seemed questionable. Thomas's moral line might have damaged the profits from rent and that, after all, was the point of Shanghai, was it not?

A small portion of the inventory reads '2 x opium shop in Canton Road property, property with Soochow women 10 houses'. These have a thick line drawn through them with 'SOLD' printed above it. The original number of properties was 1,485. The final figure was 1,462. Twenty-three were sold during the process of collation: ceasing to own a property was sometimes the easiest way to deal with unpalatable tenants.[15] Whatever the reasons for Iveson & Company's failure to conform completely with Thomas's demand of 1888, resolution had, at least, been reached by the close of 1890.

On 4 January 1892 Joseph Alexander, Secretary of the AOSSOT, wrote a letter to Thomas:

Dear Mr Hanbury,

I have received from a member of our Executive Committee, Henry Wigham, of Dublin, whose son Leonard Wigham has just gone out as a Missionary to Chun-Riang for the Friends' Foreign Mission Association, some extracts from a letter just received from Leonard Wigham written at Shanghai.

In the letter he speaks of having visited an opium den 'or rather palace', and goes on to say,

'Most of these in Foochow Road are owned by Europeans, some of the largest being the property of a Mr Hanbury who is a member of the Anti-Opium Society, and who is confidently affirmed here to be a Quaker, though I rather doubt the last statement.'

About 18 months ago I saw in one of the Anglo-Chinese papers a paragraph to the effect that you had given instructions that all the opium dens on your property were to be closed. I was informed by George Gillett that this was the result of information brought to him by Alfred Dyer, and which he had passed on to you, as to these dens. I hoped, therefore, that this was the end of the matter. It appears, however, from Leonard Wigham's recent letter that such is not the case.

I do not presume to suggest what course you may think right

to adopt as regards your Agent, who appears thus to have set at nought your instructions, but I feel bound frankly to tell you that it does not seem desirable, as far as I can judge, and Henry Wigham evidently feels strongly on the matter also, that we shall continue to print your name as that of a member of our Executive Committee, seeing that this sort of things continue to exist. I have heard from more than one source of the serious scandal that is brought upon our cause by these circumstances, but as I had hoped the scandal had been put an end to 18 months ago, I have not thought it my duty to say anything to you upon it. I should be very sorry to have to bring the matter before the Committee at its next meeting in the form of a proposal that your name be no longer printed in our list, and, therefore take the liberty of suggesting that you should kindly send me your formal resignation.

> With kind regards
> I am
> Yours truly
> Joseph G. Alexander[16]

The stink of opium had billowed up once more from the bilges of Thomas's Shanghai properties. As Alexander implied, gossip had been circulating since at least 1890. Thomas's reputation for integrity, as a committee member, as a gentleman and as a Quaker, had been severely questioned. The storm had passed in November 1890, but now, barely 14 months later, the waters around Thomas were troubled once again. Alexander's unquestioning conclusion that the only course of action open to him, as Secretary of the AOSST, was to ask for Thomas's resignation is an indication of just how compromised Thomas's reputation had become in the eyes of some of his contemporaries. Leonard Wigham's evidence had been taken, not as a fresh allegation that warranted a new investigation, but simply as confirmation of Alexander's worst fears. For Alexander, Henry Wigham's passing on of his son's claims had brought to fruition the seeds sown in 1890 by Dyer. It was this haste, the peremptory and assured proclamation of a guilty verdict that incensed and upset Thomas. Thomas was not cowed, however. The tone of Alexander's letter seems to suggest that he anticipated a quick and discreet capitulation by Thomas, but this was never likely. On 9 January Thomas wrote to Sir Joseph Pease, refuting the allegations completely and requesting the satisfaction of appearing at the next meeting of the committee to prove his innocence of the charges. He had asked Dyer and Gillett to be present for the meeting, 'at which I have already called on Mr Henry Wigham to meet me face to face and then and there apologise and retract.[17] Thomas also offered to pay the AOS-SOT one hundred pounds if there was any proof of his owning an opium den or palace.

The content of Thomas's reply to Alexander has yet to be revealed, but the content and tone of Alexander's second letter are in marked contrast to his first:

I am truly glad and thankful to hear from you that the reports current at Shanghai which have been forwarded to me through Leonard Wigham are untrue. As you tell me you have a complete answer to these reports, I think it will be better not to mention the matter to the Committee tomorrow… I fear I acted precipitately in suggesting your resignation…[18]

The meek and conciliatory style of this letter makes for an

illuminating comparison to the trenchant prose of 4 January. Alexander still sought a swift conclusion to the matter, but now to rather different ends. Thomas, however, had no intention of allowing either Alexander or Wigham to retreat in good order. Thomas had been libelled and had been the subject of slanderous gossip as well. The opportunity for a public avowal of Thomas's honesty and moral rectitude was not going to be renounced to save Alexander's blushes.

On 11 January Thomas had written to the Committee of the Friends' Foreign Mission Association to bring to their notice the 'false and scandalous libel' promulgated by one of their missionaries. Thomas wrote of his 'indignation of when I read these words penned by Leonard Wigham and which constitute the atrocious libel I complain of as false and wicked'. Thomas's anger was all the more keenly felt as he had been a member of the committee of the AOSST ten times as long as Henry Wigham and was from a Quaker family of the very oldest pedigree. Thomas again called for a special meeting to be called, offered to forfeit one hundred pounds and asked that Henry Wigham make a public retraction of his accusations.

Next, a series of telegrams and letters passed between Thomas and Henry Wigham himself. As far as Wigham was concerned, he had simply furnished the secretary with his son's report and the matter had since been resolved. Thomas's response was: 'I decline to hush it up.'[19] Thomas was determined to make the subject as public as decently possible, in order to scotch the rumours of gross hypocrisy over opium once and for all.

In the end, however, Thomas never got the public declaration of his innocence that he desired. The Friends' Foreign Mission Association sent a polite but slightly bewildered reply: Henry Wigham had withdrawn his allegation and it was a matter for the AOSSOT rather than for the Association. While expressing deep regret at the pain caused by charges brought by one of the Association's ministers, Watson Grace wrote on its behalf: 'I hardly see how we as an Association are responsible for the letters our missionaries write to their relatives.'[20]

The AOSSOT managed to avoid the promised open confrontation between Henry Wigham and Thomas Hanbury. There was a full retraction, but then Wigham felt that he had done nothing terribly wrong. He had been made aware of some information and had passed it on, privately, to Alexander. Thomas had to satisfy himself with a slightly begrudging letter of apology, rather than the drama of a committee meeting. This may not have been quite the manner in which Thomas would have wished to achieve it, but at last Wigham's letter put an end to the accusations over Thomas and opium.

In 1890, in a letter that Thomas had written to George Gillett after learning about Dyer's allegations, he had concluded that, 'short of going out myself to Shanghai, I do not know what more I can do'.[21] This was indeed to prove to be Thomas's only remaining option. On 27 June 1893 he and his three eldest children, Cecil, Hilda and Daniel, left for Shanghai, via the United States and Japan. The trip provided an opportunity for a happy compromise between Thomas and the three children, offering them the opportunity of seeing something more of the world and giving them a flavour of the travel that Thomas so loved. Thomas was thrilled to be able to share these once familiar places with his dear children. The trip also allowed him to carry out a thorough inspection of his property and business interests in Shanghai. By design or coincidence, the party arrived in Shanghai the day before official celebrations began, marking the passing of 50 years since the founding of the British Settlement in 1843, a brief passage of time in the long history of the city, but one that had seen unprecedented changes. The *North China Daily News* declared, in the course of its report on the Jubilee Ceremony held on 17 November 1893, that:

The presence of the Governor of Hong Kong, of Admiral Sir Edmund Freemantle R.N., and a large number of guests, including one, Mr Thomas Hanbury, who was celebrating the 40th anniversary of his arrival in Shanghai, and who marked his presence by the munificent gift alluded to in Mr Muirhead's address, added *éclat*.

The trip to Shanghai also permitted Thomas to see the trees on the Bund, the broad promenade along the river that he had planted in 1865–6 and 1870–1. He visited the Chinese Hospital and the Agnes Gutslaff Hospital, both of which he had helped to administer and to finance. On 24 November he accompanied his daughter Hilda to the prize-giving at the Thomas Hanbury School and Children's Home. The school had been built thanks to Thomas's donations of land and money, opening its doors in 1872. The pupils were specifically 'Eurasian', children who, at this stage of Shanghai's sexual merry-go-round, were the products of Chinese mothers and European fathers.

Whether such relationships were based in a brothel or in domestic bliss, they were understood to be part of Shanghai life and were accepted as such by the majority of the city's residents. Take, for instance, Sir Robert Hart, one of Britain's great successes in China, who became Inspector General of the Imperial Maritime Customs, and was heaped with decorations by both the Chinese and the British governments. Every nation sought his advice on matters pertaining to China. Thomas, too, referred to Hart in his lectures on China, as the man 'who has done more for China than any European who ever went to that country'. Hart had three children by his Chinese mistress by the end of the 1850s.[22] The children of these relationships were not always as easily accepted as the relationships that brought them life. The Thomas Hanbury School educated those 'Eurasian' children who had either been abandoned or declared ineligible, for reasons of race, money or propriety, for entry to the European schools, but whose parent or parents wished to have them educated in European rather than Chinese culture.

The school was in a magnificent building, a simple but elegant single-storey structure skirted with verandas and balconies. A small chapel with a tiny wooden bell-tower was attached to one side. On 24 November Hilda distributed the prizes and Thomas delivered a short speech to the children. He praised the great achievements of the children in Shanghai, told them about his schools in Italy and spoke of how much better the pupils in China were performing than those in Italy. The Italians, Thomas said, possessed 'greater genius' than any other 'race' in Europe, but they lacked 'the perseverance of the English': the two characteristics combined together would be unbeatable.[23] The obvious implication was that a mixture of the English and Chinese 'races' would have even greater potential.

The visit to the Eurasian school had a greater significance for her father than, perhaps, Hilda knew. These Eurasian children were not the first children born in China whose education Thomas had been involved in. His old *comprador* from the early days in Shanghai, Chan Laisun, had fallen on less profitable times. One or two bad decisions had robbed him of his early promise and by the mid-1860s the future did not appear to be decked in silver for the Chan family. Thomas agreed to pay for Chan's two daughters, Lina and Annie, to travel to England and be educated there at his expense. The girls lived with the

Hanbury family at Clapham and were sent to a nearby school for young ladies. They stayed for two years, opening Thomas's eyes to the very limited education available to most middle-class English girls. Dancing, drawing and music were the key subjects in the curriculum. Understandably, perhaps, the Chan girls took rather more delight in social gatherings and dresses than in the expansion of their intellects, much to Thomas's disappointment. After the girls' return to China Lina went on to marry a Scot, William Buchanan.

A boy had also left Shanghai with them in 1866. His name was Gnokee Chan, but he appears to have been no relation of Laisun and his girls. His father, once a wealthy merchant, had been bankrupted by the rebels and pirates who plagued lawless China in the 1850s and 1860s. Thomas had taken pity on Gnokee Chan, who was then aged about 12, and promised his father to give him a good education in England. Thomas became very fond of Gnokee, who, like Lina and Annie, lived in Clapham with Thomas's parents. Gnokee returned to Shanghai in 1869 and took up a position at Kung Ping, working for Thomas.

Thomas felt a very strong bond between himself and Gnokee, having rescued the boy from destitution, and fed, clothed and educated him. The relationship was one akin to that between godfather and godson. Thomas hoped that Gnokee would not only prove a great asset to Kung Ping but also become a completely trustworthy aide in Shanghai. Gnokee would be there to negotiate any particularly delicate arrangements that Thomas might require. However, Thomas's faith in Gnokee was utterly shattered in 1873, when he began to receive distressing reports about Gnokee's behaviour at work and at home. Shocked, Thomas waited until the evidence against Gnokee was quite overwhelming. On 18 December that year he felt forced to write a devastating letter to his young *protégé*. Of all the surviving letters written by Thomas, this one to Gnokee contains perhaps the rawest and most injured expression of personal feeling:

> It is eight years since I first took you at the request of your father, had you taught at Mr Fryer's school, clothed you, fed you, sent you to England, had you educated there with the sons of gentlemen, under the care of a kind and most Christian woman, Mrs Ward, you had everything you could want and were cared for by my mother + sister as if you belonged to our family, again I paid your passage out to China, gave you a place in our office, and opened an honourable career to you by which you could earn a living and have a prospect of one day being well off...
>
> Now when you might if you had behaved properly have been getting very useful and have been repaying the years of care and great expense of years, I find you turning round and behaving with the blackest ingratitude. I must believe what everyone says and that is you are guilty of cruelty and neglect of your young wife, disobedience and insult of your father-in-law, gross debauchery and wickedness in frequenting brothels in the Foochow Rd and elsewhere, often staying out very late at night or not coming home at all, disgraceful peculation to your employers, by extracting squeezes from contractors and last robbing me the best friend you have ever had or are likely to have...
>
> One thing that makes me so angry is that while pretending to be very repentant, you write me the most bare-faced lie in the following words which I copy from your note –
>
> 'I have not spent a single cash foolishly.'
>
> Though this is the last letter I will write to you I cannot go on with it, never has anything distressed me more than your turning

out badly and proving yourself as ungrateful…'

Thomas did not write unconsidered phrases, nor was he accustomed to exaggerate, or use emotive language. Most of his writing is shorn of emotional content. The sense of hurt and loss here seems likely to be as true an expression of Thomas's unconcealed emotions as one is ever likely to read. The depth of the great care and love that Thomas could bestow on those around him becomes apparent only in its betrayal. Just how profound that love could be is demonstrated in a letter that he wrote to Iveson the following day. He tells Iveson about the letter he had just sent to Gnokee and asks:

> will you please write me what effect it has on him, how he takes his discharge and what he proposes to do in the future.
>
> I very much regret being unable to devise some plan to give Gnokee a further chance for repentance and reformation… when you receive this and find he has really turned over a new leaf and he has been guilty of no new tricks such as those you describe I hope you will take some little interest in trying to get him a place as a copyist or some position…[24]

Gnokee's behaviour did not improve. If he had not been married, and had not stolen from and defrauded Thomas, then Thomas's reaction might have been very different. He would probably have harangued Gnokee for his debauched excesses, but he would not have despaired of him. Thomas knew very well the temptations available to young men in Shanghai. He had seen many others follow a similar path to the one taken by Gnokee. A Shanghai missionary is said to have commented: 'If God lets Shanghai endure, he owes an apology to Sodom and Gomorrah.'[25] Thomas himself, of course, had spent nearly 13 years, from the age of 21 to the age of 33, as a single man in that vice-ridden city. His letters home had frequently bemoaned the lack of suitable female company. However profound his religious and moral beliefs, it must have been maddening for a bachelor to live in the Devil's playground for so long without succumbing to the sins of the flesh: maddening and impossible.

With Gnokee's dishonesty and fraudulence now undisputed, all his previous duties had to be assigned to other members of the firm. There was one regular payment made privately on Thomas's behalf by Gnokee, which Thomas now had to explain to Iveson. The payment was made to a Chinese woman, Lysung, for the maintenance of her son, Ahsu. Ahsu was Thomas's eldest child. On 11 December 1873 Thomas wrote to Iveson to explain:

> My reason for not giving you particulars of these payments before and asking you to make them was partly on a disinclination to acknowledge frankly a liaison of a few months standing I contracted eight years and a half ago, the only folly of that kind I was guilty of during my stay in China, and partly because I did not like to trouble you with such things.
>
> The payments that Gnokee have been making for me are as follows –
> $30 per quarter to the Eurasian School for the schooling of Ahsu…
> $40 a month to his mother, Lysung, living rent free in my Shanking Road property…
> As regards the boy Ahsu, I intend to give him a first rate education in Europe. Gnokee wrote me that his mother has agreed that he shall come here, he is now seven years old and therefore fit to come…

Lysung, Ahsu's mother, vacillated over the terrible choice that Thomas put before her. She recognized that her son's future potential would be vastly enhanced by a European education. Thomas was offering Ahsu an extraordinary opportunity that they both agreed could only be of great benefit to him. She was, however, set against leaving China and did not want to be parted from her only child. The reasons behind her disinclination to leave China are not recorded, but they are easy to imagine. She would have been completely dependent on Thomas for every single aspect of her life, in a continent thousand of miles from her homeland. It is quite likely that she had never even left Shanghai before.

From Thomas's letters it is possible to see that Lysung's domestic arrangements were far from simple. Thomas provided a house for her, in which her mother, her brother and his wife also lived. Lysung supported her mother. They seem to have had a strange relationship. Thomas refers to her as 'the old woman calling herself mother to Lysung'[26] and 'to this woman extorting money from Lysung'. It is hard not to wonder at what troubles had occurred in Lysung's life and childhood, what would have led her to accept a possible impostor as her mother. In the state of anarchy that had held sway in China for so long, tragedy was commonplace. This 'family' would have been enthusiastic for Lysung to stay in Shanghai. Through Thomas Hanbury, Lysung housed them for free. Her position may also have been complicated by gambling debts, of which she had a history. Thomas was absolutely determined that their child should be educated in Europe.

By the end of 1874 a decision had been reached and in early 1875 Ahsu was put on board the steamer S.S. *Provence*, bound for Marseilles. Ahsu was then about nine years old. Lysung remained in

China and her son travelled to France unaccompanied. A stewardess was promised money in Marseilles if she looked after him. The entry in Thomas's diary for 5 March 1875 reads:

> 7am. S.S. *Provence* arrived with little boy Hoong Ahsu, alias Charles on board.
> Paid stewardess fr.200 for the care of him during the voyage.
>   Left with him + KAH + Enrichetta Orengo 3.45 pm train for Paris.'

The initials 'KAH' denote Katharine Hanbury, Thomas's wife. It is possible that Thomas had not told his wife the precise details of Ahsu's provenance. My own belief, however, is that Katharine knew exactly whose son Ahsu was, although when Thomas might have told her that their eldest son, Cecil, was not Thomas's first male child is not known. Thomas mentions seeing Ahsu during his stay in Shanghai with Katharine. Katharine's presence at Marseilles may be taken as evidence for Thomas's intrinsic honesty, but it demonstrates most powerfully Katharine's strength of character and generosity of spirit. The qualities of goodness and intelligence that drew Thomas to Katharine are made abundantly clear at this point in their married life. Katharine never failed her husband or their children.

The party arrived in Paris and checked into the Hotel de Nice. They called on Mr and Mrs Ortmans, old and much trusted friends of Thomas's from his days in China. Paris was to be the home of Ahsu, or Charles Sidney as he was referred to from now on, for the next eight years. On Sunday 7 March he was left in the care of the Ortmans. They had two sons of their own and it was in this family home where Ahsu was to live for most of those eight years. How any of the protagonists in this drama felt, or what they thought, is unknown. Thomas and Katharine left as early as possible that Sunday. This was not necessarily planned. They had received a telegram informing them that Daniel Hanbury, Thomas's dear brother, had fallen very ill in London. Thomas and Katharine rushed to be at his bedside. Thomas's diary entry for Sunday 7 March reports, in Thomas's typically sparse and undescriptive prose, their leaving Ahsu and setting out for London. In the bottom corner there is an uncharacteristic and darkly cryptic phrase that may reveal something of Thomas's feelings. The two words may have been added later, after reflection on the events that followed. They read: 'Table turning'. It is the only occasion in the 40 years' worth of Thomas's diaries that this expression is used. It carries with it a fatalism similar to that characterized by the Wheel of Fortune, the notion of external forces against which mortals have no power. Just over two weeks later Daniel, Thomas's beloved brother and closest ally, was dead. Thomas was a cool, unsuperstitious rationalist and it is these traits that make those two words so remarkable. It is tempting to think that, at the moment that Thomas wrote those two words in his diary, always so spartan in its content, he felt a guilty association between the arrival of Ahsu, the fruit of his brief capitulation to the flesh, and the cruel reversal of fortune, the death of Daniel.

Thomas's diaries do not offer a complete record of his life. They are very rarely expressive of emotion. Often they only hint at events of huge importance to Thomas and sometimes they do not record those events at all. Yet from the diaries it is possible to see that Thomas often visited Ahsu in Paris, as he passed through on his way between La Mortola and London. It was a journey that Thomas made three or four times a year. The mentions of Ahsu are not frequent, but the Ortmans were visited regularly. The entry for 25 July 1878, for instance, reads: ' Many hours at Exposition with Ahsu.' On 12 July 1880, Ahsu, or Charlie, paid what appears to have been his first visit to La Mortola: 'Mrs. Ortmans Ernest + Fernand + Charlie with us most of the day.' It seems that Ahsu was a good scholar and met his father's high expectations. In the back of Thomas's diary for 1880 he listed the prizes won by his son that year: 'Corneille's Plays, *Astronomie* by Desdouits, *Chimie* by Foullon, *Science a Travers Champs* by Maugeret'. The inclusion of this list denotes some pride in Ahsu's success, and the books reflect an interest in the arts and a talent for science. None of his other children have any similar prizes recorded.

The end of 1881 saw Ahsu return to Shanghai for the first time. He was back in Paris by April 1882. Then, in October 1883, while Thomas and Katharine were in England, Ahsu became very ill. The following is the complete series of entries in Thomas's diaries for the dates shown:

Sat 20th October 1883. Alarming telegrams received this day from Dr Natta dated 19th and from Dumas at Vichy regarding the state of Charlie Sidney(Ahsu). I telegraphed to Paris + Ernest Ortmans started at once for Vichy.

21st October. Recd. E, Ortmans telegram stating that Charlie is nearly dying.

22nd October. Further telegram from E.O. re. C.S.

23rd October. Charles Sidney (Hung Ahsoo) son of Lysung died at Hotel Bellencourt, Vichy. Ernest Ortmans being present. Dr Baldo of Aurole and Dr Nicolas attending. 2.45 was the time of his death.

24th October. Cecil came from Sunningdale. We met him at Waterloo + K, I, H. Sharpe + he lunched at the Radcliffes, then

went to the Fisheries Exhibition + then returned to Hollywood.
Charlie's funeral at the protestant cemetery at Vichy. Ernest
Ortmans attending.
25th October.
26th October. Wrote to China announcing Charlie's death.

It is quite impossible to gauge Thomas's emotional response to the
death of Ahsu, his eldest child, or how he felt as he took young Cecil
out from Sunningdale (his boarding school) while Ahsu was being
buried. The frigid tone should not be perceived, however, as a reflection of an absence of emotion on the part of Thomas. The tones of
his diaries are not confessional. The entries are spare in their content
and almost devoid of emotional expression. They do not represent a
record of Thomas's feelings: after all, there is a great deal of evidence,
for example in his letters to his wife and to his children, that he was
a loving and affectionate man.

One cannot help but reflect, in the absence of detail, on the
inevitable moral hierarchy of birth: on the prep school boy enjoying
his day out with his parents while the ceremony was taking place in
Vichy. Thomas had done far more for Ahsu than one might expect of
a man from his era, but there is a profound sadness in Ahsu's lonely
burial, thousands of miles away from his mother Lysung. The names
'Ahsu', 'Charlie' or 'Charles Sidney' never appear again in the diaries
of Thomas Hanbury. Yet Thomas's charitable commitment to the
'Eurasian' school named after him remained life long.

# Chapter Ten
# A decorated father

Gertrude Dymond, who was Katharine Hanbury's half-sister, was a frequent visitor to La Mortola. On 28 March 1882 she wrote a letter describing two visits by Queen Victoria to the gardens and the palazzo. The letter also contains this descriptive snapshot of Thomas's family:

Thomas and Katharine are leaving this lovely Mortola very early, partly for the children's sake who seem to want another change after their illnesses. All look pale except Dan, who is the jolliest little roundabout of six years, dressed generally in a sailor suit, which suits him greatly. He has a perpetual smile and says such funny things. He does lessons regularly with the elder ones + behaves very well; indeed they are all such nice mannered children in spite of seeing so much company and getting a good deal of notice. Cecil was ill the day I came. He is tall + clever + devoted to his Papa and getting very learned in the names & specialities of plants. He has such a sweet expression, which is like Katie, & yet he is not much like her. He is a very dear boy. Hilda is also very tall & thin, & makes shrewd remarks. She is more quick than Cecil & a nice gentle girl – Baby is a sweet-sensitive little fellow.

As to our dear Katie, she is as simple and quiet as ever, and if distinguished guests come to her, it is not that she seeks distinction – and she is equally kind and cordial to all, and makes no talk about it. And it seems to me the beauty of it, that all can enjoy here from the highest to the lowest, the combination of nature and cultivation. It is likely the Queen wishes to see it, as much as any one else, & in this simple way Katharine takes the honour conferred upon her.[1]

Thomas and Katharine had four children: Cecil, born in 1871; Hilda, born in 1872; Daniel, born in 1876; and Horace, born in 1880. These children had two extremely devoted and loving parents, and La Mortola offered them a huge, varied and happy playground. They swam, fished, sailed and kept their own gardens. Thomas was always keen to keep them amused and stimulated with trips, walks and expeditions. In 1880 he had a tennis court built for them. He was also determined that they should be disciplined in their studies, habits and finances. The strong Christian faith that was central to the lives of Katharine and Thomas was also engrained in their children. Regular pocket money was paid out, with preferential interest rates being given by Thomas for those who chose to save rather than spend.

You will find a number of kisses enclosed in this letter, if you get someone to throw them up in the air and then hold your face up, they will flutter down on to your cheeks, lips and eyes. And some are for baby Hilda.[2]

This excerpt from one of Thomas's letters is a beautiful illustration of the tender affection and love that he felt for his children. They never lacked attention, thought or care from him. As the boys reached their teenage years they were sent to boarding school in Britain. Summers were spent there increasingly often too. For all his conservation of the wild life at La Mortola, Thomas and his boys loved shooting, and would spend weeks in Scotland bagging anything from rabbits to deer. Hilda stayed by her parents' side, although she was attending private lessons. Thomas would have been the last to admit to favouritism, but his daughter was his constant companion at La Mortola and he took a special delight in her. From 27 June 1893 Thomas took Cecil, Hilda and Daniel on a round-the-world trip across the United States to Japan, China (as mentioned in Chapter 9) and Ceylon (now Sri Lanka). They returned to Italy in February 1894. This was a generous gift, but it also demonstrates how much Thomas enjoyed the company of his children and how keen he was to expand their horizons. Yet, for all this love, Thomas's relationships with his children did not always develop in the manner of his choosing. Years of controlled investment had brought Thomas vast wealth, but it brought him some losses too. Children, Thomas was to discover, could prove an equally uncertain investment.

It is difficult to ascertain the exact nature of the relationship between parents and their children. There does seem, however, to be a theme of paternal control running through the lives of Thomas's children. It is a control that speaks of great love, but it is also an exertion of authority and judgement. The course of Thomas's own early adult life in Shanghai had been determined by his desire to accumulate a fortune. Wealth was the means by which he would be able to enjoy a comfortable life with his wife and children while performing charitable works. A family was the goal. Success would then breed success, but Thomas felt that some degree of management was required.

Cecil Hanbury was the most intelligent of the three boys. He was sent to Fettes College in Scotland, not, perhaps, a natural alternative to the Riviera. From Fettes he went to Cambridge. His widow, Dorothy, wrote of his subsequent career:

> At first he wanted to go into the Diplomatic Service, but Sir Thomas, who had other views, would not allow it. Then his thoughts turned to Parliament… This idea was also contrary to his father's plans for him…
>
> When he was about twenty-two sir Thomas insisted on his going into the family business, which he did much against his own inclination…[3]

Throughout this period Cecil's mother, Katharine, gave him all her support. On 3 October 1896 she wrote to Thomas begging him to recall his son from China, where he was far from happy. Cecil left Shanghai on 22 May 1897. In April 1898 he accepted an offer from Lord Salisbury of an unpaid post as an attaché to the British Embassy in Rome. Cecil's political career had begun at last, and with his father's support. Influential friends of Thomas's, such as Sir William Thistleton-Dyer, had been vital in securing the post. Thomas also gave him considerable financial support: having lent Cecil £10,000 as capital to enter the partnership of Ward & Hanbury, Thomas later gave it to him outright on his 29th birthday.

Shortly before Cecil was dispatched to Shanghai there had been a matter of the heart that might have played an influential role in Thomas's decision to send his eldest legitimate son out East. The name 'Riri' appears in Thomas's diary for the first time in 1894. This young lady stayed at La Mortola for a week in December that year. There then occurs a most curious entry for 14 January 1895, which simply reads: 'Cecil spoke to me.' This may mean simply that Cecil had not spoken to Thomas for an unusual period of time; it may mean instead, or as well, that they spoke about something Thomas preferred not to write down even in his diary. In April Thomas paid a visit to Riri's mother, the Marchesa Maglioni. The entry for the following day reads:

13th April Genoa. With Cecil to see Marchesa Maglioni + Riri.
Pressed to name time for the marriage of Cecil + Riri – said not this year – left for La Mortola...

Thomas was not keen for his son to marry quite yet. Cecil was 24 years old; Thomas had been 10 years older at his own wedding. *His* bride had been a Quaker:

15 May – Serious talks with Cecil about his future. Cecil left for London via Genoa, he was to see the Maglionis at the latter place. From Genoa Cecil left for London.

He next met his father in Folkestone, where they stayed for two days. After they had both returned to London Thomas wrote:

17th June 1895 Folkestone to London. Cecil wrote to Riri finally breaking off his engagement.

A month later Cecil was sailing for Shanghai. Cecil finally married at the age of 43, in 1913.

The romantic lives of Thomas and Katharine's children never ran entirely according to their father's wishes. Daniel married his cousin Sylvia Dymond, daughter of his Aunt Gertrude, the lady who had been charmed by the 'jolliest little roundabout' Daniel when he was six. Thomas and Katharine dearly loved Sylvia, but Thomas was unhappy with the match, partly because Katharine and Gertrude had the same father, known to both Daniel and Sylvia as Grandfather Pease. However, after many 'serious talks', and attempts to provide spiritual and medical advice, Thomas realized that the couple were not to be dissuaded from their chosen course. On 11 December 1901 the Hanbury family met in Dorset. Thomas's diary entry reads:

> To attend the marriage of my dear son Daniel to Sylvia Dorothea, only daughter of M.G. Dymond, nee Pease. To take place tomorrow at the church of Langton Matravers Nr Swanage. I strongly disapprove of this marriage.

Daniel and Sylvia were to enjoy a very happy marriage, and gave Thomas and Katharine two very healthy grand-daughters. They lived in Alassio and were frequent visitors at La Mortola. Whatever Thomas's feelings on their marriage, he adored their company. Daniel was the only one of Thomas's children to marry in his lifetime.

Horace Hanbury met Beatrix Morgan Browne on board a ship bound for Shanghai in the winter of 1904–5. In early March 1905 Thomas and Katharine received letters asking for their consent to Horace becoming engaged. On 14 April, however, it emerged that 'Horace felt doubts'. Telegrams were exchanged between Shanghai and La Mortola, and on 15 June the impending marriage was announced in the *Times*. Further indecision followed, and the couple returned to La Mortola and Menton. The engagement was ultimately broken off on 17 January 1906. Horace returned to Shanghai, leaving a heartbroken Beatrix with her mother in Menton. It is noteworthy that Beatrix continued to visit and stay with Katharine and Thomas long after her engagement to Horace had ended. Thomas took a lot of trouble over her, taking her out daily in his car for local excursions. Thomas was now an old man of 74 and his health was beginning to fail. In early 1905 he began to experience fainting fits. Such dramas were a further drain on his health. Horace married Beatrice Souter in Shanghai in October 1907, seven months after his father's death.

Hilda proved even more unfortunate in her romantic attachments. An incident took place in November 1890 that had a lasting effect on Hilda and was of such disturbing significance to Thomas that his usual brief diary entries are replaced by long descriptive passages that fill four pages. Hilda had an unwanted suitor, a young man named Philip Sewell, who was Horace and Daniel's tutor:

8th November Spoke sharply to Sewell about his undue attentions + received his thanks.

Hilda said 'Papa what a fool Mr Sewell is, I cannot make out what he is driving at.'

The matter appeared to have been dealt with but three days later Sewell began to behave in an untoward and peculiar manner:

11th November Evening after dinner Katharine, Hilda and Sewell in drawing room. TH in his study.

Katharine told Sewell not to keep talking so much to Hilda, he jumped up and said then I will do this and he attempted to kiss her but was repulsed, Katharine scolded him but did not tell me. Sewell retreated to the schoolroom. K. found him there in depressed state appeared to have been weeping.

12th November Sewell wrote a letter to Hilda asking her to come for a walk in the garden after breakfast; she went and there told him that she did not care for him. Sewell told Katharine in the schoolroom of what Hilda had said. Sewell came to me and admitted that he had misconducted himself + had written a letter I presumed of apology. Hilda gave me this which I found to be a love letter.

Sewell and the boys went to Garian where S. had a sort of paroxysm of madness.

Told Sewell in eve that he must leave.'

Thomas relented the next day and told the tutor he could remain until the Christmas holidays if 'he conducted himself with strictness and propriety'. Sadly, Sewell's 'paroxysm of madness' developed into sustained bouts of manic behaviour. Thomas could not allow him to remain in the house with Hilda and the boys: Sewell had to go.

However, rather than returning back to England, Sewell decided to travel in Italy. Thomas was now seriously concerned about Sewell's mental health. On 15 November Thomas travelled with Sewell to Genoa and booked adjoining rooms at the Hotel de Londres. Thomas then discovered him wandering about the hotel at 4.30 am. Later that morning Thomas got hold of Sewell's wallet and called for medical advice. He managed to persuade Sewell to travel to Turin with a good friend of Thomas's, Professor Otto Penzig. Meanwhile, Thomas telegraphed Sewell's brother, who lived in Whitby, asking him to come to Turin. The next day Thomas returned to La Mortola and Sewell took the train to Turin. By 18 November both parties were back in Genoa: Sewell had escaped from Penzig but had been met at Genoa station by a forewarned friend, Cesare de Galleani. Thomas and Katharine returned to Genoa, arriving late at Sewell's hotel, checked in, and retired to bed:

19th November Roused at 2 am by porter. Sewell in great state of excitement, chattering and disturbing occupants of No. 11. Got him into our room No. 4 and K and I endeavoured in vain to quiet him, he menaced me several times and eventually I had to call one porter and then another to remain in the room + restrain him. K staid too while I locked the door on the outside as he repeatedly tried to escape. This awful state of affairs continued till 7 am when I went for Penzig.

At about 10 am we got him off to the Meconomia.

About noon his brother Joseph arrived from Whitby + approved of all I had done.

Painful scenes at the Meconomia when I, Galleani + Joseph called there + saw him.'

The next day Thomas and Katharine, both exhausted, returned to La Mortola to find that their daughter had fallen into a state not dissimilar to Sewell's: 'Hilda in a very excited state talking of going off to Genoa'. For the next three days Hilda remained in 'an hysterical excited state', depriving Thomas of at least one night's sleep. By 23 November, however, Thomas was able to write 'Hilda better' in his diary.

No other single incident in Thomas's life warrants a comparable density of writing in his diaries. It takes up four solid pages, twice as much as its nearest rival. This is not to suggest that the Sewell affair was therefore the most important event of his life. It is undeniable, however, that it was a very difficult period for Thomas and Katharine, and deeply disturbing to Hilda, their adored daughter.

Hilda's matrimonial fortunes were not gilded. She eventually married after her father's death and had one child, who died tragically. During Thomas's lifetime Hilda seems to have been dogged by disappointments and poor health. When Cecil left for Shanghai in 1895 Hilda was unwell and in bed: he bade her goodbye and 'gave her some advice about Gurowski'. A month later Cecil, having received a letter from Hilda, noted: 'Hilda dismal again rather – poor girl she wants helping in life.' In early August 1896 she went with her father to Bayreuth. The entries for 4–5 August in his diary read:

> Serious talk with Countess Doenhoff about Hilda + the offer of Prince Ludwig Louvenstein. Agreed that Hilda should stay here three weeks more.
>
> Talked again with Ctsse Doenhoff about Hilda + wrote her a letter on the subject of a proposed engagement.

The proposed engagement never came to fruition. Next, Hilda became very much attached to Lord Lovatt, but, it is alleged, Thomas forbade the match because the Lovatts were staunch Catholics. It may well have been her close friendship with the Lovatts that drew Hilda towards the Church of Rome. The ending of her relationship with Lord Lovatt because of Thomas's objections perhaps fuelled her interest in the faith. Whatever the reasons, in 1905 Hilda, single and 33 years old became once again the subject of a unique entry in Thomas's diary. He drew a rectangle that almost fills the space for 14 August 1905. Its thick and sombre outline is heavily marked in black ink. Inside this box he wrote:

> Formal admission into the Roman Catholic Church of our own dear daughter Hilda Beatrice to our own great grief and regret at the convent manningtree.

Thomas did not use phrases such as 'great grief' in an unconsidered way. The sadness he felt may have been a form of mourning for more than sectarian differences. He may have perceived that Hilda's embrace of Catholicism constituted a rejection of his paternal authority. Indeed, although Christianity remained a central part in all their lives, none of his children maintained an allegiance to the Quakers.

The cultivation of a garden, with appropriate plants correctly planted, fed and watered, is a pursuit blessed with an agreeable element of predictability. Any unlooked-for eccentricities can be weeded out. With the minimum of care a sapling will grow into a tree similar to its parents. It will live on long after the man or woman who planted it has died. Gardeners can plot and direct the future lives of plants with a degree of control, and satisfaction, that may elude them as parents. The one plant recorded as being introduced to the garden by Hilda is *Caltha polypetala*, a vigorous marsh marigold. She brought it to La Mortola from the gardens in the Vatican City. The spiritual dimension of a botanic garden can take many forms.

Thomas's attitudes to children and their futures led to his close involvement with the local communities around La Mortola from the very beginning. Two days after he took his fateful boat trip from Menton to La Mortola on 25 March 1867 (see Chapter 5) he had already given 200 francs towards aid for Italian schools. On 3 May 1867 he talked to the local curé, Père Vesco, about setting up a school for the girls of La Mortola and six days later he employed his first schoolmistress, a 15-year-old called Feliciana Muratore. In June 1869, as Thomas prepared to leave for Shanghai with Katharine, he left instructions for the running of schools in the villages of Latte and Grimaldi as well. As has been discussed earlier (also in Chapter 5), the public education system in Italy was of a fragile constitution, dependent on the local landowner or commune for its existence. He found, that from the outset, no charitable action went unnoticed. In March 1868 Lorenzi sent him a translation of an article in a local newspaper published in San Remo. It was a eulogy to Thomas and his efforts on behalf of the children of La Mortola:

> Of such deeds all praise is too insignificant. It is unnecessary to add that they have excited the universal gratitude of the village and the admiration of the town of Ventimiglia.[4]

The author goes on to complain that to admire, rather than act, is all that the Ventimiglia commune seems capable of. The article suggests that such municipal slackness in providing schools was unpatriotic and un-Italian. Education was a highly political issue.

The new school at Ciotti was opened in June 1870. Thomas was unable to attend its official opening, as he was still in Shanghai, so it fell to his brother, Daniel, to preside over the ceremony. Daniel's discomfort because of the unavoidable task of public speaking was worsened by the lack of tea at the celebrations:

> As I was cheated out of my tea and had to drink instead a glass or two of wine, I passed a very uncomfortable night and have all this day been confined to the sofa with diarrhoea – thanks to rhubarb & magnesium, followed by chalk mixture and laudanum I am feeling better and hope to be nearly well tomorrow.'[5]

Thomas was now responsible for providing the teachers, as well as the furniture, books and other equipment, for four schools. Each village had to contribute a building, or rather a room, in which the lessons might be conducted. These 'classrooms' could be squeezed into an empty cantina in a trattoria or, in the case of Grimaldi, into a room above the village's public ovens. In poor areas, with no tradition of lay education, there were simply no school buildings. Since 1859

the communes had been obliged by the new but not yet wholly
united Kingdom of Italy to provide public primary education, but a
lack of funds and zeal had meant that in Thomas's district little had
been achieved outside Ventimiglia itself. The villages were thus
dependent on charity. Thomas was not the only wealthy man in the
district: what caused him to stand out from among the established
families was his charitable largesse.

The arrangements for housing the schools were clearly unsatisfac-
tory. Three of Thomas's schools, those of Grimaldi, Ciotti and La
Mortola, were within reasonable proximity to one another. On 18
April 1878 Thomas proposed amalgamating them into a single
school, to be established at La Croce, the cross above the gardens. The
land belonged to the Prince of Monaco, who was persuaded to donate
the site to the commune. Thomas then built a school and a house for
the teachers at a cost of 30,000 lire. The school was opened in 1880.
Thomas paid for the teachers' salaries and all other expenses. George
Muller, resident for 40 years in Menton, wrote of the Croce school:

> After a long pull up the dusty road… we reach the schoolhouse
> (Scuola Hanbury), where the children of the surrounding villages
> receive sound, gratuitous, non-sectarian instruction. The posi-
> tion is most beautiful, the house commodious, the schoolrooms
> cheerful and liberally provided with all the appliances that make
> instruction comparatively easy and pleasant. Mr Thomas
> Hanbury has done, and is doing, a vast amount of good not only
> within his immediate neighbourhood but over a wider area, and
> all in the most unostentatious way.[6]

The new school at Latte was opened in 1890, although it was still
partly under construction. Its official inauguration took place on 1

January 1892. The school was a triumph of design and construction, for which the British architect W.D. Caroe was responsible. Every detail was minutely considered, from the way in which the natural light would fall across the pupils' desks to the building's ability to withstand earthquakes. The teachers were each provided with a two-bedroomed residence in the grounds of the school. The final construction costs came to 150,000 lire. Thomas also contributed a third of the teachers' stipends. He could rightly claim that his school at Latte was 'superior in solidity, convenience and architecture to any rural school in the provinces of Porto Maurizio'.[7]

Any doubts over the perceived importance of education to Italy's aspirations as a European nation, or any questions about Thomas's understanding of the importance of schools in the landscape of Italian politics, are answered in Thomas's inaugural address at the opening of the new school at Latte:

> We are all here today to enjoy a unified Italy. This is for your freedom and your future growth, but even as we rejoice at this, we must not be blind to the huge amount of work still to do nor cease to be shocked, when we look at other countries, such as France, Switzerland and Germany, where so many children already receive education, while here we have millions unable to read or write.
>
> Permit me to emphasise this point: I feel that it is vital to concentrate on the instruction of the mind in order that the words uttered by your great patriot Mazzini: 'We have made Italy but we have yet to make Italians' may not lose their power and simply become a cliché.[8]

Thomas's interest in the schools that he founded was not confined merely to their construction and financial upkeep. He examined the pupils of each school in person every year. These examinations were far from being cosmetic exercises, for Thomas presented a written report on his findings to each of the teachers. In July 1880, for example, he tested the children at the old Latte School, offering five prizes for the best performances in each of the following categories: reading, writing, arithmetic and personal cleanliness. He was pleased with the children's showing in most of the subjects, but was critical about their reading:

> Too mumbling, droning and indistinct. I hope at the end of the year to find both boys and girls reading with a loud, clear, ringing and distinct utterance, paying proper attention to emphasis and stops.[9]

However, the role of stern examiner was one that Thomas was happy to put aside. Once a year the children were invited up to their benefactor's palazzo for a variety of games and frolics, followed by a large tea. The children at these gatherings were sometimes not even from Hanbury schools, as the entry in Thomas's diary for 2 June 1898 demonstrates:

> School treat. About 30 or 40 girls came from Ventimiglia + about ten from Mentone – see-saw, rocking horses, tug of war + other games. Refreshments in the Topia.

The management of the schools proved to be far from trouble-free. In May 1881 Thomas 'spoke severely to the master' after irregularities in opening the school. Two weeks later he called a meeting of parents and found that, of the 27 present, 15 had complaints against the schoolmaster. In 1887 he felt forced to dismiss Signor Panizzi from his post as schoolmaster 'in the interest of public decency'. In June 1889 two of the schoolmistresses, Signoras Frontero and Adami, were asked to resign because of their 'ever-recurring quarrels'. Two other schoolmistresses who caused Thomas some recurring problems were Anne and Maria Crudeli. Thomas's diary entry for 31 December 1894 is typical of his penchant for understatement: 'Handed notice to Anne & Marie Crudeli for end of the scholastic year – scene ensued.' The 'scene' was to continue for a number of years, as the sisters sued Thomas for loss of earnings. Their case was eventually dismissed.

Thomas's commitment to Italy's future through the education of its people was not restricted to primary schools. The plant collection that he was amassing in the garden at La Mortola had brought him to the notice of eminent botanists throughout Europe. It was through such a connection that Thomas first met Professor Otto Penzig, head of the school of botany at the University of Genoa (whom we have already met earlier in this chapter). Their friendship led directly to Thomas's funding of the Instituto Hanbury, a new school of botany, in the botanic garden of Penzig's university. The building was designed by the grand Italian architect Carlo Canavese, whose bill alone came to 97,500 lire. The Institute is a stately testament to Thomas's determination to contribute to Italy's resurgence in Europe. The inaugural ceremony took place in September 1892, amid Genoa's celebrations of the 400th anniversary of its most famous son's most famous deed, Columbus's discovery of the Americas. The Institute's first official duty was to host a conference on European botany, attended by more than 60 botanists. A highlight of the gathering was, of course, a visit to the gardens at La Mortola.

Thomas's efforts to further the educational cause in Italy had not gone unnoticed. Thomas was made a Cavaliere, in 1868, and then, in 1890, a Commendatore of the Order of Saints Maurizio and Lazarro, an ancient award of the Knights of Malta and the highest Italian honour conferred on foreigners. In 1885 and 1888 he became Cavaliere and Commendatore, respectively, of the Order of the Grand Cross of the Crown of Italy. In 1892 he received a gold medal from the Minister of Public Instruction. All these commendations were overshadowed, however, by a fiasco that followed the inauguration of the Instituto Hanbury at Genoa University. In September 1892 the Minister for Public Instruction, one Signor Martine, put Thomas's name forward for elevation to the Italian nobility, as a Marchese. This was a huge honour and it delighted Thomas. The proposal was accepted by the King, and became the subject of considerable publicity, as well as congratulations in the press and from Thomas's friends. So widely acknowledged was the honour that letters began to arrive addressed to Marchese Hanbury.

A few months after the announcement of the decoration, the Giolitti government, which had been instrumental in promoting Thomas's new title, collapsed. Thomas waited some time longer for the completion of the formalities deemed necessary before the conferral of the title of Marchese became official. The silence and inactivity of the Italian authorities were finally broken in December 1895, when Thomas was told that letters concerning his family, his coat of arms, heraldic deeds and various certificates were required before any further progress could be made. Thomas delivered the correct documents on 19 February 1896, but when they were returned to him they had with them a letter informing him that the title was not to be granted after all. Thomas was furious and felt embarrassed. He had not sought the honour: he had been informed of its award and now it had been mysteriously denied him. In a letter that he wrote to Professor Penzig his indignation and sense of injury are clear:

> There is no expression of regret, no reason given, I am left in ignorance whether I have done anything wrong; whether the certificates were unsatisfactory, whether I was expected to change my nationality; or whether for such an immense honour (?) I was expected to pay a large sum of money or lastly whether some hidden enemy contrived this as a studied insult. I feel like asking his majesty to take back and cancel the other Orders conferred on me by himself and his late Father.[10]

On 3 October 1896 a Genoese newspaper, *Caffaro*, published a virulent article on the subject of 'Marchese Hanbury'. The force of the article was directed against the Crispi government, but it used the award of the title to Thomas as the exemplar by which the government's deficiencies were, it claimed, exposed. The fact that it had been the Giolitti government, not that of Crispi, that had nominated Thomas indicates the hysterical inaccuracy that pervades the piece. Thomas is referred to as 'a Croesus reposing on the shores of the province of Porto Maurizio'. The schools he had built become 'princely residences', while the means by which he acquired his wealth is made more scurrilous than even the accusations of involvement in opium dealing (discussed in Chapter 9): 'The name of Hanbury is very well-known on the Riviera and also among his African slaves…'[11]

A full apology and retraction were printed in November, but Thomas remained deeply wounded. In a letter dated 29 December 1896, from Marquis di Rudini, President of the Chamber of Deputies and friend of Thomas, the intricacies of the Marchese affair were made more explicit. After reading the letter, Thomas wrote 'It is now sufficiently clear that the Prime Minister considers that an hereditary distinction should not be enjoyed by an Englishman, though why it was proposed by the Representative of the King still remains a mystery'.[12] Thomas had privately printed an elegant pamphlet, documenting the farrago. It was sent to all his closest friends and went some way to ease his damaged pride:

> I send you my Pamphlet marked 'Private & Confidential.', it might be entitled the strange story of an Italian title.
>
>     I think you will agree that the Italian government has not treated me with much courtesy.[13]

What might have represented the ultimate recognition of all Thomas's generosity, leadership and industry on behalf of education in Italy came to be a source of embarrassment and disaffection for him. His British contemporaries were somewhat dismissive of the value of an Italian title anyway.

Thomas's commitment to the people of La Mortola and its environs did not falter, for such rewards had never been his aim. Others sought recognition of his generosity. Prior to 1892 and the offices of the Minister for Public Instruction, another official body had proposed a similar honour for him. In 1891 the commune of Ventimiglia sent a request for Thomas to receive a formal title for his unstinting charity and aid to the local people. In 1895, when Cecil Hanbury boarded the ship that was to take him to his undesired sojourn in Shanghai, Thomas gave him some words of advice. The journey to the docks had been made in an uncomfortable silence between father and son. Thomas had spoken to some of the other passengers in the carriage, but to the son he was forcing to go to Shanghai he said little.

Just before leaving the ship and bidding Cecil farewell, however, he gave some final advice to his son: 'Those men succeed who do not expect too much in life.'[14] It may seem strange advice from a man of such ambition and drive as Thomas, yet his final triumph, which distinguished him as a man of accomplishments and of substance, was to have its roots in an unexpected source.

From the garden's earliest days it had become an attraction for visitors to the Riviera. Even before Thomas arrived in Italy La Mortola, its cape and the dilapidated palazzo had provided a picnic site for those staying in Menton. Any diversion of a 'wholesome' nature was seized upon with gusto by those who overwintered on the Riviera. The delights and distractions available to these 'tourists' were very limited. Thomas quickly found that his garden, even in its infancy, was a magnet for all manner of visitors to the area. His brother Daniel wrote to Dr Spruce on 10 May 1869, complaining that the garden was already becoming 'too favourite a drive for the numerous English visitors to Mentone'.[15] European royalty was also taking an interest in Thomas's garden, the suite of the Queen of Prussia, for example, having visited on 5 May.

Social visits and excursions made in carriages formed the backbone of all 'respectable' recreation. Monte Carlo offered all sorts of entertainments to the swelling ranks of Riviera tourists, but its sordid reputation for immorality kept the God-fearing well away from its clutches. It is hard, perhaps, to understand the common distaste expressed by many visitors, residents and natives of the Riviera for the presence of the Casino and its tributaries at Monaco. Thomas abhorred gambling. So strongly felt were his objections that he attended an anti-gambling meeting as far away as Nice to show his support. This excerpt from a travel book of 1908 expresses the disgust for Monte Carlo and its habitués that was common among many of Thomas's contemporaries:

> one sees types of humanity that in a few minutes rob the place of its beauty; the sunlight becomes garish, the gardens a vulgar display, and even the sea seems to lose its dignity. Pickpockets, loudly dressed women of many nationalities and men representing the depraved element in the moneyed classes of all the countries of Europe, turn Monte Carlo into a spot which cannot fail to be repugnant to the observant who find nothing attractive in the marks of a vicious life.[16]

The gardens at La Mortola, made by a wealthy Quaker philanthropist and botanist, offered an excellent alternative both to boredom and to the iniquities of Monaco. La Mortola thus became part of the Riviera circuit. During 'the Season' Katharine began to host occasional 'days at home', serving refreshments to visitors. Thomas noted that on a single day, 11 March 1881, 300 people descended on the gardens, carried there in 69 carriages and on 18 donkeys.

'This will long be remembered as the whitest day in the annals of Mortola…': so begins the special memorandum that Thomas wrote after Queen Victoria's visit to La Mortola, which took place on 25 March 1882. This and a subsequent visit made three days later confirmed absolutely the place of La Mortola in the social diary of all who came to the Riviera. Some of the impact of such a royal visit may have dissipated today, but in 1882 the event was of such perceived consequence and honour that Thomas had a marble plaque placed on the walls of the palazzo as a constant memorial to it. Gertrude Dymond's letter is most insightful as to the great furore and awed reverence that accompanied the Queen's public activities, however spontaneous they might be. The second visit to La Mortola appears to have been rather more impromptu than the first. The royal entourage:

> sent a message she was coming again in 20 minutes and she wished to be quite undisturbed. It so happened that Tuesday is Katharine's 'at home' day and there were even more visitors than usual who had to be hastily bustled up to the upper salon, while the lower one was again prepared for her Majesty.
>
> Thomas blew his Japanese horn with which he calls the men, and sent [them] to clear the gardens; the confusion was considerable, as everyone had lost daughters or husbands or parasols etc. Old Canon Philpott was so deaf and had to be made to understand, & poor old Mrs Best, in spite of two crutches, got all the way up the marble staircase! When it was found which way the Queen went, and that she was not coming into the house immediately, all the visitors came out from their retreat and went away by another path.[17]

An extract from the Queen's own journal entry for 28th March 1882 shows how successful Thomas's management of the evacuation had been:

> Drove with Beatrice, Jane C. & Ld. Bridport, again on the Italian side. We got out at La Mortola, (no one but the gardiner being there) & walked about looking at the marvellously beautiful flowers and plants, all blooming most brilliantly.

The Queen's journal entry for 5 April the same year includes the following:

> M- Hanbury having himself brought over a basket full of the

most wonderful, rare flowers, I sent for him up from the Lodge, & spoke to him. He is a Quaker & his granduncle old W. Allan, was a friend of my Father's & also of Uncle Sussex. His wife is a cousin of the Corndavon Peases...[18]

Thomas Hanbury had been noticed and he had been received.

On 3 August, on the Queen's invitation, Thomas arrived at her residence of Osborne House on the Isle of Wight. He stayed there for a single night and, having surveyed the gardens, enjoyed an interview with her at 11 o' clock that evening. Thomas's introduction to the Queen–Empress's court, and to the titular ruler of what was then the most powerful empire in the world, had been made possible by his garden. Without this botanic accoutrement Thomas would have been nothing more than another rich, retired merchant and property dealer.

The garden at La Mortola gave Thomas an entrée into what must have seemed to him to be a most rarefied social stratum. The Prince of Wales had first visited La Mortola in 1878, four years before his mother's two visits, and was to return three more times before inviting Thomas to spend a weekend at another royal residence, Sandringham, in 1899. After Queen Victoria's death Thomas had a 15-minute interview with the new King Edward VII, as the Prince had become, on 4 June 1901. A little over a month later Thomas went to Marlborough House. He recorded in his diary that day: 'Invested there by the King with the Insignia of Knight Commander of the Victorian Order': Thomas was now *Sir* Thomas Hanbury. Officially this great honour had been awarded to him for his work in China and in Italy.

Thomas had begun his garden because of the love of plants that he shared with his brother Daniel. La Mortola's popularity with visitors was an unlooked for by-product. It is difficult to imagine his social elevation without the essential primary boost provided by the garden at La Mortola. It provides the sort of example that socially aspirant garden owners delight in. For some a garden can serve as a hallmark of acceptability, an outward display of worthiness. Gardening, like reading, is often portrayed as an activity of unimpeachable reputation, morally improving to all who partake in it, but the element of self-improvement is one that attracts many to gardening.

Thomas first saw Wisley on 14th September 1889, when he visited its owner, George F. Wilson. There was no house to speak of, just a small cottage that was more of a shelter than a residence. In August 1903, after Wilson's death, Thomas offered to buy the garden on behalf of the Royal Horticultural Society (RHS). The importance of this gift to the RHS is self-evident today. To understand its significance as it was understood in 1903, I went to the society's library, housed at its offices on Vincent Square in London. The Lindley Library, as it is known, is the finest horticultural reference library in Britain, and it is open to members of the RHS and non-members alike. Its value is not measured in terms of books alone.[19] At the end of the 19th century the RHS was being riven by a dispute that endangered its internal stability. Its garden in Chiswick was under constant threat from encroaching and polluted London, and the horticultural school there had faltered. The decision to acquire a 'new Chiswick' was not a simple one to make. At the same time the flower shows that were administered by the RHS and represented another of its primary functions were split between halls in the Temple and Holland House, neither of which belonged to the RHS. Desperately in need of a new garden *and* a new central exhibition hall, the RHS was faced with a dilemma. It could afford only one of these and the members of its council were not unanimous in their judgement of its priorities.

On 30 September 1903, nearly two months after Thomas had offered Wisley to the RHS, he wrote to Sir William Thistleton-Dyer:

> I saw Chiswick yesterday for the first time at a lunch given by the RHS. The garden did not impress me favourably, the fellows in fact said they (the Gardens) were worn out.[20]

Clearly his knowledge of the difficulties at Chiswick was far from being first-hand. The problems that the RHS were facing had been brought to Thomas's attention by Miss Ellen Willmott, a great friend of his who owned three large gardens over the course of her life. Her pursuit of horticultural excellence was uncompromising and ultimately ruinous. The last garden she acquired was that of Boccanegra, which lay across the bay at Latte, opposite La Mortola. Her frequent visits to the Palazzo Orengo had inspired her to produce a 'mini-Mortola'. Her gardens and their obsessive management proved to be destructive. When Thomas visited Boccanegra in 1906, a year after she had bought the property, he found 50 men at work in the garden. Miss Willmott ended her days penniless and lost in eccentricity. It was however, Miss Willmott who helped Thomas to deliver Wisley to the RHS. When Thomas made the offer of Wisley, on 4 August, Miss Willmott attended the Council meeting in a supporting role. The minutes record that she 'explained various points connected with the garden'.[21] The proposal to accept Thomas's gift was seconded by Sir Henry, Baron Schroder, who distinguished himself by securing the lease of Vincent Square for the RHS. In July 1904 King Edward and Queen Alexandra opened the new Horticultural Hall.

The dilemma had been solved, but there remained some, such as Thomas's friend Sir William Thistleton-Dyer, Director of Kew, who were implacably opposed to the notion of Wisley. Thistleton-Dyer thought of Wisley as a white elephant that would be lost in its provincial location out in Surrey. This was an opinion that Thomas himself had shared only a year previously. Wisley's rural location was a crucial element of the gift, however, as it allowed for expansion, and G.F. Wilson had always maintained Wisley as an experimental garden, which made it ideally suited to further the aims of the RHS. Thomas was not worried by Thistleton-Dyer's objections, and they proved to be a source of amusement between him and Miss Willmott. Thomas was careful to point out to Thistleton-Dyer, in a letter dated 4 October 1903, the superiority of Wisley over both Chiswick *and* Kew:

Perhaps you fail in not giving Wisley the credit of being out of the smoke and soot of London which cannot be said of Kew or Chiswick. Where else within the same distance of London could 60 acres of freehold be found with admirable soil and an abundant water supply, a garden already made by an eminent man and secured at the moderate price of £5,000.[22]

On 14 November 1903 he wrote to Sir Joseph Hooker:

The late Mr G.F. Wilson's property at Wisley consisted of 59½ acres freehold in which was included his well known garden and a small house. I gave this in August to the R.H. Society; the society is left perfectly free, only if it fails to keep it up, the property passes to Kew.[23]

Thistleton-Dyer's strong disapproval of Wisley's location amid woodland and farmland was to prove misguided. The garden at Wisley now covers an area of 240 acres and the RHS has more than

300,000 members: room to grow was vital. The presentation of Wisley to the RHS secured Thomas's lasting and profound influence on the future of horticulture. Wisley has become one of the most important European experimental gardens, trialling garden plants, fruit and vegetables for both professional and amateur nurserymen and gardeners. It was from Wisley that the RHS School of Horticulture became internationally renowned. In September 1903 Thomas was awarded the Victoria Medal of Honour in Horticulture and on 20 April 1906 he received the prestigious Veitch Memorial Medal for his services to horticulture.

# Chapter Eleven
# Inveni portum…

There is a handsome photograph of Thomas, a portrait made in the last few years of his life. It was taken just outside his palazzo: Thomas in a light country suit, white-whiskered and seated in a deck chair. He looks quite the archetype of the genial old gentleman. Behind him, on the portico of the palazzo and out of shot of the camera, runs an inscription. It reads:

*Inveni portum,*
*spes et fortuna valete,*
*sat me lusistis*
*ludite nunc alios.*

A translation might run:

I have found harbour,
expectation and fortune farewell,
you have toyed with me enough,
play with others now.

The lines were taken from LeSage's poem 'Gil Blas'.
La Mortola, whatever the outward appearances of flesh and

masonry, did not constitute a farewell to expectations or the vicissitudes of fortune for Thomas. Such an *adieu* could come only with a withdrawal from life and from activity, which Thomas would never even have considered. His dealings in property, investments and currency never ceased. In his 70s he was still looking to new schemes, offering £5,000 for shares in the Pacific Island Company, which removed guano from Ocean Island to sell as fertiliser. By 1906 even Katharine had been supplied with a thousand of these shares. Thomas could not stop himself; he could not retire from a passion. Even on his trip to the Holy Land in March and April 1889 his gimlet eye for property never dimmed. His diary entry for 31 March includes: 'Called on Mr Frutiger + endeavoured in vain to negotiate for purchase of land containing reputed tomb of our Lord.' The years 1905–6 saw Thomas involved in the negotiations for Ellen Willmott's property, Boccanegra (see Chapter 10) and even as late as 6 June 1906 he was buying yet more land in Italy. If he had ever exclaimed '*Inveni portum…*' he would have assessed the sheltered harbour for its potential as a property investment before he had even set foot ashore. Thomas never ceased to build on what he had: inactivity was unthinkable. Relentless increase for the future was a process that had become as natural to Thomas as photosynthesis is to a plant, and it went beyond his financial and business interests. It was a characteristic exemplified by his concern about, and control over, the lives of his children, and La Mortola too is a testament to his zeal.

The unending task of creating the garden at La Mortola was well-suited to Thomas. It could never be finished, and it demanded a perpetual investment of time, money and care. When Thomas bought La Mortola he was 34 years old: more than half his entire lifespan would be spent making it a botanic and horticultural jewel. The human element of the garden alone determined that the day-to-day running of La Mortola would be anything but a retirement. The curators, head gardeners and gardeners kept Thomas very much engaged in life. The evidence from Ludwig Winter's time at La Mortola demonstrates this point clearly, yet the distractions by no means ceased after Winter's departure in 1875. During 1876 and early 1877 Thomas had become increasingly exercised by the scale of theft from his garden. Thomas warned his staff that he was well-aware of what was going on, yet the stealing continued. Thomas discovered that the culprit was Otto Zacharias, the head gardener, with the connivance of his assistant Rutschi. Carl Keller, the gardener to the Prince of Monaco, was also involved but his exact role remained unproven.

As Thomas's diary records, events at La Mortola could be brutal. On 12th July 1888 he noted: 'Sebastiano Viale murdered last night by stab in groin by Girolomo Biancheri. Nicola Viale badly wounded.' Dinter, the curator/head gardener who replaced Cronemeyer after the latter died suddenly in 1892, proved to be no stranger to violent behaviour. He was dismissed on 29 March 1896, two days after an incident mentioned in the diaries: 'Salvai attacked by Dinter in the cottages of Giacomo.' As late as July 1904 Thomas was mediating between his superb curator, Alwin Berger, and his head gardener, Joseph Benbow. The row, which lasted for a week, had arisen over that ever-contentious subject, water supply. The plants were to prove rather less obstreperous.

Inevitably, given Thomas's generative nature, the dynamic that drove his garden was that of production and use. On its most basic level this began with fruit. The annual production of citrus fruits was considerable. They were sent to friends and relations or sold, either for local consumption or to Allen and Hanbury for their essential oils. Thousands were sent annually to Clapham and even to Shanghai. The collection of citrus trees that Thomas acquired was the finest on the Riviera in his time. Daniel Hanbury's botanic connections resulted in nearly 30 varieties being sent from Sicily alone in 1875. That same year Thomas collected pips from an orange tree in Rome, known as St Dominic's Orange. Daniel wrote in *Pharmacographia*:

> There is strong evidence to show that the orange first cultivated in Europe was the Bitter Orange or Bigarde. The orange tree at Rome, said to have been planted by St Dominic about AD 1200, and which still exists at the monastery of St Sabina, bears a <u>bitter</u> fruit; and the ancient trees standing in the garden of the Alcazar at Seville are also of the variety.[1]

(The pips made a healthy tree, a descendent of which now grows in the garden of Carolyn Hanbury, who makes a superb ice cream from its fruit.)

Other citrus trees were planted for different reasons. The Buddha-fingered Orange, an extraordinary fruit, has lost its spherical shape, and looks deflated and flattened. Its growth process is irregular and produces the finger-like segments that give the plant its name. It was a particular favourite of Thomas's, as he explained to Sir Joseph Hooker:

> It is very fragrant + used in China by Chinese ladies who hold it in their hands or have it on the table near them when receiving visitors, much as a fine embroidered handkerchief might be used in other countries. I got the plant over the year before last from China. It is now flowering + has set some fruit.[2]

Oranges were certainly not the only fruit at La Mortola. A broad selection of useful plants was trialled in the gardens. Through his support of the Agnes Gutslaff Eye Hospital in Shanghai, and through the interest in medicinal plants encouraged by Daniel, Thomas looked to grow a plant whose exceptional properties have since been the reason for a great deal of suffering and political hypocrisy. On 26 November 1884 Thomas wrote to Thistleton-Dyer at Kew:

> Oculists seem much excited now over the properties found in *Erythroxylon coca* + I would very much like to try and grow it at Mortola. Where could I get seed or a young plant?[3]

Thistleton-Dyer obligingly sent him some seeds in February 1885, but, to Thomas's disappointment, none of the plants flourished. Any hopes Thomas might have had for cocaine production in Liguria were dashed.

Another stimulant that interested Thomas was *khat*, the leaves of an evergreen tree, *Catha edulis*, which are chewed or smoked, and are most commonly used in East Africa and the Arabian Peninsula. In the popular lectures that he occasionally gave in Bordighera and Menton Thomas extolled the virtues of this plant as an alternative to alcohol for the working man.

The gardens at La Mortola were experimental in their conception. They were meant to look to the future, rather than simply indulging in a green reverie. As Daniel wrote to Spruce on 30th May 1869:

> It is not unimportant to introduce another good fruit into the Riviera. The loquat (*Eriobotrya japonica*) is valuable both for its elegant appearance and for ripening its fruits just at the season when there is little else to be had.[4]

Experiments did not have to be unattractive: what is apparent is that it was not only the usefulness of a plant but also its beauty that was of interest to Thomas. The fruit of the garden, the succour provided by La Mortola, was not exclusive to the trencherman or the botanist: it was for the eye and the soul as well. A letter to Daniel from the scientific botanist Gustave Thuret, concerning the planting of succulents and dated 28 December 1872, makes much of the effect made by the plants:

Certainly, I would be very happy if I could be of some use to your brother in the planting of his garden. But in that regard, the advice of Mr Winter would be better than mine – besides you know my opinion of the gardens around here. I find that they look to imitate those in the north too much and that not enough is made of succulent plants.

Rather than spreading them here and there, I would like to see them used en masses. If I had had a garden graced with south facing terraces, I would certainly have tried out this system. Large blocks solely composed of Aloes, Opuntia, Cereus, Euphorbia, Sempervivum, Kleinia etc, I believe, would produce a very picturesque and a very original effect.[5]

The experimentation is also in the design of the beds and planting schemes. Thuret encouraged Thomas and Daniel to be bold and original. Winter was clearly of the same mind as Thuret. As Thuret goes on to mention: 'This would not be everybody's idea of a garden', but Thomas loved these block plantings, particularly with agaves. It became a distinctive La Mortola design and certainly helped to confirm Thuret's observation about popular opinion. Thomas's garden lecture includes some of the most common complaints of visitors to

La Mortola. One begins: 'Yes, there are beautiful plants and lovely views, but it's not a garden...' This style of succulent planting may have been rather surprising to some of Thomas's contemporaries, but it has become a standard when using succulent plants in gardens. The design ethos of the Monaco Exotic Garden, for example, appears to be based entirely on this one precept.

La Mortola did not rely only on the drama of its succulent plants and its various fruits for its appeal. There were, of course, flowers as well. Thomas mentioned to Thistleton-Dyer on 18 March 1885: 'the garden is ablaze with anemones now'. In some quarters, at least since 1914, it has been suggested that the garden in Thomas's day lacked much in the way of flowering colour, so that, while it astonished visitors as a collection of plants, it was a little on the dry side visually. I think that this is a mistaken perception, promulgated by an idea of the garden in retrospect. During the 1920s and 1930s great emphasis was placed on bedding displays and the like. In comparison to such a floral carnival, Thomas's tastes may well have seemed a little restrained. However, the gardens were far from barren in this regard. A garden that lacked flowers would not be one that supplied them to others in abundance, yet Thomas loved to send boxes of flowers to his friends and relatives. In six months of 1887, for example, he dispatched nearly 300 boxes full of blooms cut from his garden. Such quantities would not have been possible in a garden that neglected floral display. In 1904 an order was placed for 62,000 plants of anemones, tulips, sparaxis and other bulbs for the gardens, hardly an appropriate order for a garden unconcerned with colour. The garden was largely ignored during the tragedy and upheaval of the First World War, and much of the vivid underplanting that had been overseen by Thomas was lost. The image of the garden in Thomas's day was slowly drained of colour and, in the mind's eye, faded to sepia. Flowers have long been an emblem of the ephemeral and their passing in a garden, of all places, should not be a cause of wonderment.

The flowers at La Mortola may have had some relevance to the steady increase of visitors that came to see the garden. The popularity of Thomas's garden did not slacken as the years passed. His receipt of a knighthood had confirmed La Mortola as a compulsory fixture in the tourists' itinerary. The height of the season lasted from January to the end of May, when the first days of summer would drive the last of the visitors northward. During this period in 1903, for example, 5,303 people visited the garden; 1904 saw this number increase to 6,351. The visitors were not simply tourists, royalty or not. The links with other botanic institutions were growing year by year, so horticulturalists and botanists from throughout Europe made use of the plant collection. Thistleton-Dyer, Hooker and Bentham all visited, as did the Quaker botanist father and son John and Edmund Baker, who were enthralled by Thomas's agaves. Kew had long been cherished as a generous supporter of La Mortola and Thomas was always keen to reciprocate any favours. He regularly offered plants to Kew and was delighted whenever he could add to Kew's collection from his own, although the traffic tended to be heavier leaving Kew. Rutschi, Zacharias and Dinter all benefited from being sent to Kew for a few months, to improve both their English and their horticultural techniques.

The collection of seed from the hundreds of plant species grown at La Mortola formed a vital element in the garden's productiveness. In 1890 Thomas sent 95 packets of seed to Kew alone and it was the distribution of seeds to botanic gardens, from Ceylon to Newcastle, that Thomas treasured. In 1886, for example, 2,596 packets of seed were dispatched from La Mortola, the majority to botanic gardens around the world. The La Mortola seed list helped to establish the garden's botanic reputation internationally. Thomas was also an enthusiastic supporter of the *Botanical Magazine*, a periodical that might lay claim to being the product of the most graceful and long-lasting marriage of erudition and beauty in the world of publishing. Not only did he stand by the magazine in times of financial worry, but his garden contributed 19 species to be illustrated and described in its pages. In 1893 Sir Joseph Hooker dedicated the 119th volume to Thomas in these words:

> My dear Hanbury, – It is no less a duty than a pleasure to offer you the dedication of a volume of the *Botanical Magazine* as a tribute to the value of your services to Scientific Horticulture in creating a garden of Exotic plants at Mentone which, in point of richness and interest, has no rival amongst the private collections of living plants in the world; and in munificently funding the 'Instituto Botanico Hanbury' in the Botanical Gardens of the University of Genoa, the early years of which are already so full of promise for the future of Scientific Botany in Europe.

The most impressive mark of Thomas's standing within the botanic community was prepared for his 75th birthday, 21 June 1907. The curator at La Mortola, Alwin Berger, had put together an album containing signed photographs of more than 150 of the most eminent botanists and horticulturalists in the world, all of whom were known to Thomas, from Medley Wood and Bolus in South Africa to William Robinson in London. The countries involved were as diverse as Japan and India. Sadly, however, Thomas was not destined to receive this great tribute:

Perhaps you have seen in the papers that our dear Sir Thomas Hanbury died peacefully on Sat. evening after only a few weeks illness.

It is impossible for me to describe to you our grief and sorrow. He will not only be missed by those who knew him intimately but by thousands of poor people.

His funeral which took place yesterday bore the best testimony in how great esteem he was held. As his body was cremated at San Remo the funeral procession passed from here all along the coast and in every place the shops were closed and the whole population joined the procession. It is said nearly 7,000 people were present.[6]

In Ventimiglia, just down from the railway station, there is a bust of Sir Thomas occupying an area in a little square, a tribute to his charity. To the left of it runs a narrow street that leads on to Via Hanbury. It is hard to miss, as its entrance is marked by Bar Hanbury, whose presence is proclaimed on a large, illuminated sign, an appropriation of the family name that might have surprised the Quaker Thomas. Nearly 100 years after his death few of the remaining monuments of Thomas's generosity and industry have survived unchanged. The school at La Croce was deserted for years before someone decided to renovate it. I presume it was for a private residence, but the money ran out a couple of years ago, so now it is just an anonymous shell. The handsome school at Latte has been sold by the local council and successfully converted into a private house. It is a wonderful building that exudes a solid charm, but it is difficult to inspect it at close range without alarming its residents. At the University of Genoa the Instituto Botanico Hanbury is still home to the department of botany.

The Palazzo Orengo is as beautiful and simple as ever. It now provides offices for the administrative staff that runs the garden. La
Mortola was given to the Italian state in 1960 by Lady Hanbury. The
University of Genoa currently runs it. The garden retains tremendous
poise and some areas are still maintained to a high standard. I have
met some of those who work there, and there is no shortage of skill
or of love for the garden. There are a tremendous number of talented
and passionate people in and around the garden, who feel strongly
about its future. Despite this, the garden carries with it, like a top
note to the heady scent of pine and sea, a sense of limbo. La Mortola,
for Thomas, was not a static park in which he had stationed himself.
It thrived, it produced and it was useful. As I left preparations were
being made for discussing the potential for some sort of horticultural
school at La Mortola, surely an idea that Thomas would have adored.

This book was never intended to be the definitive biography of Sir
Thomas Hanbury. Not every element of his life and character has
been included: we have no space to cover his interest in local archae-
ology, his charitable works after the earthquake of 1887, his gifts to
libraries in Italy and England, or a number of other topics. Many
details of his private and family life remain undiscovered. I have
attempted, instead, to provide a sense of the man Thomas was and of
why he made the garden at La Mortola.

The garden was not a peacock garden or a show garden, but it
became the most visited private garden on the Riviera, and resulted
in Thomas's social elevation and eventual knighthood. The garden
was intended for Thomas to enjoy along with his brother Daniel, but
Daniel died just eight years after La Mortola was begun, while
Thomas lived for another 32 years. Things did not always go to plan.
The iron-shod morals that are so often presented as the core of

Thomas's being slipped occasionally. He was a man, surrounded by opportunities for love and for money, and endowed with a strict sense of right and wrong. He expected a lot from those around him, but the demands he made on himself were greater. At times he may have failed to live up to those self-imposed moral principles. Such occasions were few, however, and it is clear that Thomas walked a straighter line through venal, licentious and violent Shanghai than most. One contemporary who had worked at Kung Ping wrote of Thomas: 'His fair treatment of the Chinese was in flat contrast to that of almost every Englishman in the Settlement...'[7]

Thomas's generosity and considered charity attest his compassion. On the day of his cremation, as the funeral procession passed through the quiet streets of Ventimiglia, a man was heard to sigh: 'We have lost our father.' Thomas had spent his life producing wealth, which he enjoyed both in acquisition and in possession; but he also took a great deal of pleasure in its charitable distribution.

In travelling to Shanghai in 1853 and staying there for years, Thomas can be said to have risked everything, body and soul. He returned a very rich man. He had the wealth to live comfortably, to create one of the finest gardens of the age, and to give generously and thoughtfully, in time, spirit and large amounts of money, to the future health of the land in which he lived. He remains today an example of compassionate capitalism, striving for profit, but not at the expense of his faith and humanity. His reputation among the Chinese, his alienation from other foreigners in the Settlement and the respectful mourning of his death by thousands of Italians all speak of his character. Yet he did not achieve his great affluence without cost, either to himself or to others. Without the trade in opium and the forcing of markets in China there would have been no trade at all.

Without the violence brought to bear by the armies of the British, the French and others the European traders might well have been swept into the sea. Thomas was aware of the fragile moral ice on which he had set up shop. His letter to his sister after the Battle of Muddy Flat demonstrates this. The whiff of opium and the popular image of the sharp-dealing, fast-living Shanghai traders followed Thomas. I have been told that the majority of ten-pound notes in circulation today contain traces of cocaine, so widespread is its use: Shanghai money would have had no physical evidence of opium, but its ubiquity was such that most cash was soiled.

The most insignificant details can be connected with events of great consequence. The entry in Thomas's diary for 12 January 1891 reads innocuously enough:

> To fancy dress ball with Cecil and Hilda at Theatre of San Remo.
> Appeared in Emperor's Robe + a Chinese hat.

Yet the robe was part of the loot from the infamous sacking of the imperial Summer Palace by British troops. Thomas's high moral tone was not always easy to live up to, as Thomas found himself. For all Thomas's extraordinary qualities, he was at times reassuringly human and fallible. The birth of Ahsu provides compelling evidence. That sad episode highlights the constraints and contradictions of Victorian propriety, and the conditions that it imposed on Lysung, Thomas, Katharine and Ahsu. Thomas was forced to contrive a balance between his Christian conscience and the demands of the society that he chose to inhabit.

Thomas was, of course, a more complicated man than I had anticipated. So successfully covered over was the story of Ahsu's short life that my own surprise at the discovery of the boy's existence was equalled by Carolyn Hanbury's. Shanghai had made Thomas's fortune, but it also added some unwelcome dimensions to his moral perspective. It is impossible to say how harshly Thomas may have judged himself, but perhaps such feelings produced yet further impetus for his life of unceasing industry and charity.

Gardens present themselves as a visual treat and thus are often considered from a purely aesthetic viewpoint. Such criteria can rob a garden of its context, detaching it from the people and the society that created it. No garden is an island. Ever since 1867 the garden at La Mortola has never been a free-floating entity, existing in isolation. It both depended on and reflected Thomas Hanbury, and the events that were shaping the world outside its gates. Like the Emperor's robe that Thomas wore as fancy dress, the garden was deeply enmeshed in China and Thomas's past. It was linked as well to the history of the Mediterranean coast on which it lies, and its people and their culture. This rich contextual heritage continues to be added to today. I hope that this book has gone a little way in describing the nature of Sir Thomas Hanbury and his garden at La Mortola. For all the complexities of personality and history, the beautiful soul of this garden is made of a man's love of plants. Nothing is more expressive of this than the plants themselves.

There is another sign on the roadside up Corso Monte Carlo that marks the approach to the gardens at La Mortola, which I did not mention in my description of the drive up from the sea. This sign is totally concealed from view by a young specimen of *Yucca elephantipes* that has been planted directly in front of it. If there is a plant, or a flower, that makes me think of Sir Thomas Hanbury it is the yucca. The yucca comes in all sizes, from the large *Y. elephantipes* to the small *Y. brevifolia.* Its leaves are slender and sword-shaped, and range from the glossy to the glaucous. Yuccas are familiar house plants, largely due to their relative invulnerability to human cultivation: they are survivors. The flower of a yucca is not only an object of great beauty; it is an ecological parable, a sublime fragment of natural harmony. The flowers are held in a panicle, a champagne spray of blooms mounted on a branching stem. Each individual flower is a cool, waxy composition of creamy, greenish-white bells of six petals or tepals. At the centre of each flower, like a fountain, are the upright female parts, surrounded by six stamen, in a magnolia-like Busby Berkley arrangement. The flower is beautiful, but its fertilisation is truly divine. Many species of yucca are beholden to a single genus of moth, *Tageticula* or *Pronuba*. The female moth takes the pollen of one flower to another and then pushes it down the female flower parts to the ovary. During this process the moth lays eggs in that very same ovary. As a moth larva matures it consumes some of the developing seeds, but not all. Once it is of the requisite size, the larva chews its way out of the seed capsule. It then falls to the ground and buries itself in the soil, where it pupates into a moth, before initiating the process again. The cycle of symbiosis is dependent on the moth releasing the correct number of eggs into each ovary. Too many moth larvae and there would be no yucca seeds, but without the moth the yucca would not produce seed.

After years of research into the pollination of the yucca Charles Riley published his findings in 1892. In May 1893 Thomas wrote to Daniel Morris, Assistant Director of Kew:

> It will be very interesting to try the fertilisation of some of my yuccas by means of the insect *Pronuba yuccasella* but I feel a little doubtful how the Italian govt. would (in its ignorance) view the introduction of a new insect, seeing that now they require those

persons who bring loads of potatoes from France into Italy to wash the tubers most carefully at the frontier lest the earth adhering should contain eggs of insects, more especially *Phylloxera*.

I return next month to Italy for a botanical excursion in the mountain range 30 miles north of Mortola & will then take the cocoons unless already sent.

*Yucca aloifolia* produces good eatable fruit at Mortola, tasting like blackcurrant jam with a pinch of quinine.[8]

The tiny and probably illegal Mexican moths were duly released. They fluttered into the Ligurian countryside and disappeared. The pollinating period of the yucca is brief and nocturnal. Nobody ever saw the moths again. Alwin Berger, writing in *Hortus Mortolensis* (1912), noted that during 1897–8 seed capsules of *Yucca flaccida* had been collected 'which exhibited the peculiar holes from which the larvae may have escaped'. No evidence of the activities of *Pronuba yuccasella* has since been recorded.

This is the garden that Thomas made.

# Acknowledgements

The research for, and writing of, this book took place in England and Italy. It is safe to say that, without the kindness and support of institutions and individuals in both these countries, hardly a sentence could have been written.

The Archivo Hanbury, held by the Instituto Internazionale di Studi Liguri in the Clarence Bicknell Museum, Bordighera, provided the overwhelming mass of the letters, papers and diaries that make up the heart of this book: the help and kindness of all the staff there was invaluable. Many thanks also to all the hard-working staff at the Giardini Botanici Hanbury. In England the librarians, the archivists and the Trustees of the Royal Botanic Gardens Kew, the Royal Pharmaceutical Society of Great Britain, the School of Oriental and African Studies, the Religious Society of Friends and the Royal Horticultural Society's library in Vincent Square were equally generous with their time and expertise. Thanks to Dr Brent Elliot, the RHS Librarian; and my aunt Catriona Macdonald, John Dickie, Erino Viola, Daniella Guglielmi, Letitzia Pagnetti, Helen Chattwell, Jo da Silva, Dycella Cummings-Palmer, Jim Carroll, Mike Nelhams and the wonderful Michelle 'Reedy' Read.

Special thanks to Sarah Such for her faith and guidance.

Above all, I would like to express my gratitude to Carolyn Hanbury and thank her for a happy and unique summer at Casa Nirvana. It would just be paper without her.

# Chapter Notes

I must acknowledge a great debt of gratitude to Grace Kiernan and Mauro Muratorio for their book *Thomas Hanbury and his Garden*, which blazed a considerable trail in researching the life of Sir Thomas Hanbury. Charles Quest-Ritson's *The English Garden Abroad* was also inspiring.

Some of the entries in the notes below end with abbreviated letters. These refer to the archives and, in one case, a privately published book from which material has been taken. The abbreviations are as follows:

IISL – Archivo Instituto Internazionale di Studi Liguri, Bordighera. Fondo Hanbury, cat.

KA – Extracts from the Directors' Correspondence Books, Trustees of the Royal Botanic Gardens, Kew.

LTH – *The Letters of Sir Thomas Hanbury* ed. Lady Katharine Hanbury, 1913.

PHA – Copybooks of letters, Private Hanbury Archive. Any letters not found in the chapter notes are from these books.

RPS – IRA.2001.045 The Royal Pharmaceutical Society of Great Britain.

For details of other sources see Bibliography.

Chapter One – La Mortola: Giardini Hanbury

1 Casey, *Riviera Nature Notes*, pp. 85–86.

Chapter Two – Shanghai bound
1 The chapter on tea in Hobhouse, *Seeds of Change*, is the main source here.
2 See Booth, *Opium: A History*, and Rudgeley, *The Encyclopedia of Psychoactive Substances*
3 Letter of Thomas Hanbury to Daniel Hanbury, 29 Sept. 1853, PHA.
4 *The Jubilee of Shanghai 1843–1893: Shanghai Past and Present*, revised and reprinted from the *North China Daily News*, 1893.
5 Ian Heath, *The Taiping Rebellion*, p. 7.

Chapter Three – Topside Galah
1 Letter of Thomas Hanbury to Mr Wilson, 7 Jan. 1854, PHA.
2 Letter of Thomas Hanbury, 15 Nov. 1853, PHA.
3 Letter of Thomas Hanbury to Anna Hanbury, 9 April 1854, PHA.
4 "China As I Knew It", LTH.
5 Letter of Thomas Hanbury to Samuel Gurney, 23 Feb. 1854, PHA.
6 Letter of Daniel Hanbury to Thomas Hanbury, 1–3 Feb. 1857, IISL.
7 Letter of Thomas Hanbury to Daniel Hanbury, 21 Nov. 1859, IISL.
8 Letter of Thomas Hanbury to Daniel Hanbury, 15 Nov. 1853, PHA.
9 IISL.
10 IISL.

Chapter Four – Foreign devils
1 Letter of Thomas Hanbury to Rachel Hanbury, 21 Sept. 1853, PHA.
2 Letter of Thomas Hanbury to Rachel Hanbury, 27 Oct. 1853, PHA.
3 Letter of Thomas Hanbury to Rachel Hanbury, 17 Jan. 1854, PHA.
4 See note 2.
5 Letter of Thomas Hanbury, 13 Dec. 1853, PHA.
6 Letter of Thomas Hanbury to Daniel Hanbury, 28 March 1859, IISL.
7 IISL.
8 Letter of Thomas Hanbury, 22 Oct. 1853, PHA.
9 Letter of Thomas Hanbury, 18 June 1861, PHA.
10 Letter of Mr Batchelor to Katharine Hanbury, Nov. 1913, IISL.

11 Dong, *Shanghai*, p. 22.

12 Letter of Thomas Hanbury to Daniel Hanbury, 18 Aug. 1860, LTH.

13 Letter of Thomas Hanbury, 8 Oct. 1861, LTH.

14 Letter of Thomas Hanbury to Daniel Hanbury, 19 Feb. 1861. PHA.

15 Letter of Thomas Hanbury, 2 July 1861, LTH.

16 Heath, *The Taiping Rebellion*, p. 42.

17 LTH.

18 Letter of Thomas Hanbury, 19 Jan. 1862, LTH.

19 See Macpherson, *The Wilderness of Marshes*.

20 Letter of Thomas Hanbury to Daniel Hanbury, 29 Oct. 1855, IISL.

21 Letter of Thomas Hanbury to Daniel Hanbury, 19 March 1860, IISL.

22 Letter of Thomas Hanbury to Daniel Hanbury, 17 Sept. 1865, LTH.

23 Letter of Thomas Hanbury to Daniel Hanbury, 5 Oct. 1865, LTH.

24 Letter of Thomas Hanbury to Daniel Hanbury, 20 April 1864, LTH.

25 Letter of Thomas Hanbury to Daniel Hanbury, 13 May 1865, IISL.

26 IISL.

27 IISL.

28 LTH.

29 LTH.


Chapter Five – Riviera Robinson Crusoe

1 Letter of Thomas Hanbury to Daniel Hanbury, 22 April 1866, PHA.

2 All extracts from the diaries of Thomas Hanbury, IISL.

3 Letter of Thomas Hanbury to E. Iveson, 17 April 1867, PHA.

4 Letter of Thomas Hanbury to E. Iveson, 8 May 1867, PHA.

5 Letter of Thomas Hanbury to F. Bower, 18 April 1867, PHA.

6 Letter of Daniel Hanbury to Thomas Hanbury, 8 June 1860, IISL.

7 See Mack Smith, *Garibaldi*.

8 See Clark, *Modern Italy*.

9 Clark, *Modern Italy* p. 35.

10 Letter of Thomas Hanbury to F. Bower, 20 Dec. 1869, PHA.


Chapter Six – Inspiration

1 'Daniel Hanbury: One of the Founders of Pharmacognosy", *Pharmaceutical*

*Journal*, Vol. 214, pp. 417–21.

2 Ibid., p. 417.

3 Letter of Thomas Hanbury to Brenier, PHA.

4 Title page of F.A. Fluckiger and D. Hanbury, *Pharmacographia.*

5 *Pharmaceutical Journal*, Vol. 214, p. 419.

6 Ibid., p. 420.

7 Daniel Hanbury, *Science Papers*, p. 11.

8 Ibid., p. 514.

9 *Chemist and Druggist*, Vol. 17, 15 April 1875, p. 119.

10 Daniel Hanbury, *Science Papers*, p. 10.

11 *Pharmaceutical Journal*, Vol. 115, p. 343.

12 *Chemist and Druggist*, Vol. 17, p. 119.

13 Daniel Hanbury, *Science Papers*, p. 24.

14 Letter of Daniel Hanbury to Thomas Hanbury, 18 March 1860, IISL.

15 Daniel Hanbury, *Science Papers*, p. 20.

16 Ibid., p. 24.

17 "Continental Journal", 11 June 1852, PHA.

18 Ibid., 8 June 1852.

19 Ibid., 11 June 1852.

20 Ibid.

21 *Chemist and Druggist*, Vol. 17, p. 120.

22 Daniel Hanbury, *Science Papers*, p. 26.

23 Letter of Thomas Hanbury to Daniel Hanbury, 11 Nov. 1853, PHA.

24 Letter of Daniel Hanbury to Thomas Hanbury, 1 Dec. 1861, IISL.

25 IISL.

26 Letter of Daniel Hanbury to Thomas Hanbury, 29 Dec. 1870, IISL.

27 Letter of Daniel Hanbury to Richard Spruce, 28 Sept. 1870, RPS.

28 Letter of Ludwig Winter to Daniel Hanbury 18 Feb. 1873. IISL

Chapter Seven – A garden in Italy

1 Letter of Thomas Hanbury to E. Iveson, 25 July 1867, PHA.

2 Letter of Thomas Hanbury to Batchelor, 29 Dec. 1869, PHA.

3 IISL.

4 Letter of Daniel Hanbury to Thomas Hanbury, 24 Nov. 1870, IISL.

5 Letter of Daniel Hanbury to Thomas Hanbury, 27 Nov 1870, IISL.

6 Letter of Daniel Hanbury to Thomas Hanbury, 13 July 1871, IISL.

7 Letter of Thomas Hanbury to Iveson, 10 Nov. 1871, PHA.

8 Letter of Thomas Hanbury to Katharine Pease, 11 Feb. 1868, LTH.

9 Bennet, *Winter and Spring on the Shores of the Mediterranean*, p. 38.

10 IISL.

11 IISL.

12 Letter of Thomas Hanbury to Batchelor, 29 Dec. 1869, PHA.

13 Clark, *Modern Italy*, pp. 69–73.

14 IISL.

15 IISL.

16 See Hamilton, *Bordighera and the Western Riviera.*

17 Letter of Thomas Hanbury to Sir William Thistleton-Dyer, 4 April 1879, KA.

18 Letter of Thomas Hanbury to Sir William Thistleton-Dyer, 12 Oct. 1894, KA.

19 Letter of Thomas Hanbury to Sir Joseph Hooker, 12 Jan. 1879, KA.

20 Clark, *Modern Italy*, pp. 93–96.

21 IISL.

22 LTH.

23 IISL.

24 Letter of Thomas Hanbury to Katharine Hanbury, 30 Dec. 1868, PHA.

25 Letter of Ludwig Winter to Thomas Hanbury, 2 Aug. 1872, IISL.

26 IISL.

27 Letter of L. Winter to Thomas Hanbury, 18 Aug. 1873, IISL.

28 KA.

29 IISL.

30 Letter of Thomas Hanbury to Sir William Thistleton-Dyer, 2 Dec. 1876, KA.

31 IISL.

Chapter Eight – The pitiful want of water

1 Berger, *Hortus Mortolensis*, p. xi.

2 Letter of Daniel Hanbury to Richard Spruce, 10 May 1868, RPS.

3 Berger, *Hortus Mortolensis*, p. xi.

4 Letter of Thomas Hanbury to Cuthbertson, 20 Jan. 1874, PHA.

5 See Bennet, *Winter and Spring on the Shores of the Mediterranean*, p. 188.

6 See Clark, *Modern Italy*.

7 Bennet, *Winter and Spring*, p. 189.

8 Thomas Hanbury, "General Instructions for the Management of La Mortola", Nov. 1871, IISL.

9 Letter of L. Winter to Thomas Hanbury, 18 Jan. 1872, IISL.

10 Extract first published in *Gardens Illustrated*, BBC Worldwide Publications, issue 69, Feb. 2002.

11 Letter of Daniel Hanbury to Thomas Hanbury, 10 Feb. 1870, IISL.

12 Letter of Daniel Hanbury to Thomas Hanbury, 6 Oct. 1870, IISL.

13 Letter of Thomas Hanbury to Cabagni, 12 May 1873, IISL.

14 Muratorio, *Daniel Hanbury and the British Colony of Alassio.*


Chapter Nine – The taint of opium and fruit of Shanghai

1 Letter of Thomas Hanbury to Daniel Hanbury, 4 Aug. 1853, PHA.

2 Letter of Thomas Hanbury to his father, Daniel Bell Hanbury, 9 April 1854, PHA.

3 Letter of Thomas Hanbury to Samuel Gurney, 23 Feb. 1854, PHA.

4 *Friend of China*, March 1875.

5 Letter of Richard Spruce to Daniel Hanbury, 11 Jan. 1874, RPS.

6 Dong, *Shanghai*, p. 53.

7 IISL.

8 IISL.

9 IISL.

10 Letter of George Gillett to Thomas Hanbury, 17 April 1890, IISL.

11 Letter of George Gillett to Thomas Hanbury, 28 April 1890, IISL.

12 Letter from J. Ambrose to Thomas Hanbury, 14 Nov. 1890, IISL.

13 Ibid

14 Charles Tyzack, "Friends in West China, 1886–1927", *Friends Quarterly vol.24, no.6*, April 1987, p. 255.

15 IISL.

16 IISL.

17 IISL.

18 Letter of Joseph Alexander to Thomas Hanbury, received 12 Jan. 1892, IISL.

19 Thomas Hanbury's note made of telegram sent to Henry Wigham, 18 Jan. 1892, IISL.

20 Letter of Watson Grace to Thomas Hanbury, 19 Jan. 1892, IISL.

21 Letter of Thomas Hanbury to George Gillett, 4 Aug. 1890, IISL.

22 Dong, *Shanghai*, p. 28.

23 *North China Herald*, 24 Nov. 1893.

24 Letter of Thomas Hanbury to E. Iveson, 19 Dec. 1873, PHA.

25 See Dong, *Shanghai*.

26 Letter of Thomas Hanbury to Gnokee Chan, 10 Jan. 1873, PHA.


Chapter Ten – A decorated father

1 Letter of Gertrude Dymond to M. Hogg, 28 March 1882, PHA.

2 See Muratorio and Kiernan, *Thomas Hanbury and his Garden*, p. 156.

3 See Hanbury, *La Mortola Garden*, p. 5.

4 IISL.

5 Letter of Daniel Hanbury to Thomas Hanbury, 27 June 1870, IISL.

6 Muller, *Mentone and its Neighbourhood*, p. 378.

7 IISL.

8 IISL.

9 IISL.

10 Muratorio and Kiernan, *Thomas Hanbury and his Garden*, pp. 164–65.

11 IISL.

12 Thomas Hanbury, *To My Friends*, 1897, KA.

13 Letter of Thomas Hanbury to Sir William Thistleton-Dyer, 22 Jan. 1897, KA.

14 Diary of Cecil Hanbury, 12 Sept. 1895, PHA.

15 RPS.

16 See Home, *Along the Rivieras of France and Italy*. p. 104.

17 See note 1.

18 The Queen's Journal, Royal Archives, Windsor Castle.

19 I am grateful for the time and knowledge of the RHS Librarian, Dr Brent Elliot.

20 KA.

21 Minutes of the Royal Horticultural Society, 1903, in Lindley Library, Royal

Horticultural Society.
22 KA.
23 KA.

Chapter Eleven – Inveni portum
1 F.A. Fluckiger and D. Hanbury, *Pharmacographia*, p. 125.
2 Letter of Thomas Hanbury to J. Hooker, 20 Jan. 1883, KA.
3 KA.
4 RPS.
5 Original in French:
*Certainement je serais très heureuse si je pouvais être de quelque utilité a votre frère pour la plantation de son jardin. Mais les conseils de M. Winter a cet regard vaudront beaucoup mieuses que les miens – Vous savez d'ailleurs mon opinion sur les jardins de ce pays-ci. Je trouve qu'on cherche trop à imiter ceux du nord, et partout qu'on ne tire pas assez parti des plantes grasses.*
*Au lieu de disperser celles-ci, ça et là, je voudrais les voir employé en grandes masses. Si j'avais eu un jardin disposé en terrasses tournées vers le midi, j'aurais certainement essayé le systemé. Des massifs uniquement formés d'Aloes, Opuntia, Cereus, Euphorbia, Sempervivum, Kleinia etc, seraient, je crois, d'un effet très pittoresque et très original.* (IISL)
6 Letter of Alwin Berger to Lt-Col. Dr David Prain, 12 March 1907, KA.
7 Letter of Batchelor to Katharine Hanbury, 6 Nov. 1913, IISL.
8 Letter of Thomas Hanbury to Daniel Morris, 7 May 1893, KA.

# Bibliography

**Books and pamphlets**

Ralph Austen, *A Treatise of Fruit Trees*, Oxford, 1653

J.H. Bennet, *Winter and Spring on the Shores of the Mediterranean*, London: J & A Churchill, 1875

Berger, Alwin, *Hortus Mortolensis*, London: Klest-Newman & Company, 1912

Mary Blume, *Cote d'Azur: Inventing the French Riviera*, London and New York: Thames & Hudson, 1994

Martin Booth, *Opium: A History*, London: Simon & Schuster, 1996

Roderick Cameron, *Golden Riviera*, London: Weidenfeld & Nicolson, 1975

Reverend George Edward Comerford Casey, *Riviera Nature Notes*, London: Bernard Quaritch, 1903

Desmond Chapman-Huston and Ernest Cripps, *Through A City Archway: The Story of Allen and Hanburys, 1715–1954*, London: John Murray, 1954

Martin Clark, *Modern Italy, 1871–1995*, second edition, Harlow: Longman, 1996

Richard Davenport Hines, *The Pursuit of Oblivion: A Global History of Narcotics*, London: Weidenfeld & Nicolson, 2001

Stella Dong, *Shanghai – The Rise and Fall of a Decadent City*, London: HarperCollins, 2000

W. Roger Elliot and David L. Jones, *Encyclopedia of Australian Plants*, eight volumes, Melbourne: Lothian, 1980

F.A. Fluckiger, *An Easter Holiday in Liguria*, privately printed, 1877

F.A. Fluckiger, *La Mortola: A Short Description of the Garden of Thomas Hanbury*, privately printed, 1885

F.A. Fluckiger and Daniel Hanbury, *Pharmacographia*, second edition, London: Macmillan, 1879 first published 1874

C.M. Foust, *Rhubarb: The Wondrous Drug*, Princeton, NJ: Princeton University Press, 1992

H.S. Gentry, *Agaves of Continental North America*, University of Arizona Press, 1982

H.A. Giles, *China and the Manchus* Cambridge: Cambridge University Press, 1912

Frederick Hamilton, *Bordighera and the Western Riviera*, London: E. Stanford, 1883

Sir Cecil Hanbury, *La Mortola Garden: Hortus Mortolensis*, London: Oxford University Press, 1938

Daniel Hanbury, *Notes on Chinese Materia Medica*, London: publisher unknown, 1862

Daniel Hanbury, *Science Papers, Chiefly Pharmacological and Botanical*, edited with a memoir by Joseph Ince, London: Macmillan, 1876

Sir Thomas Hanbury, *The Letters of Sir Thomas Hanbury*, edited by Lady Katharine Hanbury, London: West, Newman & Company, 1913

Sir Thomas Hanbury, *To My Friends: A Statement*, privately printed, 1897

Ian Heath, *The Taiping Rebellion, 1851–66*, London: Reed, 1994

Henry Hobhouse, *Seeds of Change*, London: Sidgwick & Jackson, 1985

Gordon Home, *Along the Rivieras of France and Italy*, London: J.M. Dent, 1908

Brian Hook (ed.), *Shanghai and the Yangtze Delta*, , London: OUP, 1998

Mary and Gary Irish, *Agaves, Yuccas and Related Plants*, Timber Press, 2000

Author unknown, *The Jubilee of Shanghai 1843–1893: Shanghai Past and Present*, revised and reprinted from the *North China Daily News*, Shanghai, 1893

Ronald King, *Tresco: England's Island of Flowers*, London: Constable, 1985

Jan Kolendo, *The Agave* Pages, at www.users.globalnet.co.uk/~jankol/main.html

Kuo Sung-Tao, *The First Chinese Embassy To The West – The Journals of Kuo Sung-Tao*, translated by J.D. Frodsham, Oxford: Clarendon Press, 1974

Audrey le Lievre, *Miss Willmott of Warley Place*, London: Faber, 1980

Dennis Mack Smith (ed.), *Garibaldi*, Englewood Cliffs: Prentice-Hall, 1969

K.L. Macpherson, *The Wilderness of Marshes: The Origins of Public Health in Shanghai, 1843–93*, London: Oxford University Press, 1987

Maura Muratorio, *Daniel Hanbury and the British Colony of Alassio*, Savona:, 2000

Francesca Mazzino, *An Earthly Paradise: The Hanbury Gardens at La Mortola*, Genoa: Sagep, 1997

George Muller, *Mentone and its Neighbourhood: The Past and the Present*, London: Hodder & Stoughton, 1910

Maura Muratorio and Grace Kiernan, *Thomas Hanbury and His Garden*, San Remo: Instituto di Studi Liguri, 1992

Mike Nelhams, *Tresco Abbey Gardens*, Truro: Dyllansow Truran, 2000

Earnest Nelmes and William Cuthbertson (eds.), *Curtis Botanical Magazine Dedications 1827-1927*, London: Bernard Quaritch, 1931

Michael Nelson, *Queen Victoria and the Discovery of the Riviera*, London: I.B. Tauris, 2001

F.B. Power, *The Influence and Development of Some of the Researches of Daniel Hanbury*, London, 1913

John Prest, *The Garden of Eden: The Botanic Garden and the Recreation of Paradise*, New Haven, CT: Yale University Press, 1981

Charles Quest-Ritson, *The English Garden Abroad*, London: Penguin, 1992

G.W. Reynolds, *The Aloes of South Africa*, Johannesburg: The Trustees, Aloes of South Africa Book Fund, 1950

Richard Rudgeley, *The Encyclopedia of Psychoactive Substances*, Boston, MA, and London: Little, Brown, 1998

Harriet Sergeant, *Shanghai*, London: John Murray, 2002

Betty Peh-T'i Wei, *Shanghai: Crucible of Modern China*, London: Oxford University Press, 1988

## Unpublished archives

Hanbury Archive, Royal Pharmaceutical Society

Archivio Hanbury, Instituto internazionale di Studi liguri, Bordighera

Directors' Correspondence and Outward Books, Archive of the Royal Botanic Gardens, Kew

RHS Council Minute Book, Lindley Library, Royal Horticultural Society

## Periodicals

*Chemist and Druggist*

*Friends Quarterly Examiner*

*Friend of China: The Organ of the Anglo-Oriental Society for the Suppression of the Opium Trade*

*Gardener's Chronicle*

*Gardens Illustrated* (BBC Worldwide Publications)

*Journal of Botany*

*Journal of Horticulture and Home Farmer*

*Kew Bulletin*

*North China Herald*

*Pharmaceutical Journal*

*Proceedings of the Linnaean Society*

*Revue horticole*

*Transcripts of the Botanical Society of Edinburgh*